Perriu

A Narrowboat Tale

Come in, my friends, as journey take
Our story for to tell
A fantasy of Witches, Dwarves
And Wizard's evil spell

As follow o'er the winding route
Words tingle and excite
As travellers meet on old canals
But who will win the fight?

So turn the pages, join the tale
Of how things came to be
Will Perriwillow get back home?
- You'll have to wait and see

By Janul

Illustrated by Gary Young

Janul Publications

Dedicated to:
Bill Buckley, my Dad
Terry Glover
Warren

With thanks to:
Toni Coleman
Barry & Jenny Wood

"Perriwillow", created by Janul Buckley, © 1980
Published by Janul Publications, © 2020

All copyrights - Janul Publications

Illustrator - Gary Young

ISBN-978-1-906921-20-0

Other books by the Author:

My Life On A Narrowboat, 2011

Narrowboat Kitchen, 2011

The Adventures Of Pirate:
Through The Lock, 2010
Pirate In The Dock, 2010
Pirate Goes To A Festival, 2010

Lines From The Heart & Valentine Verses, 2009

www.janulpublications.com / publications@janul.com

Table of Contents

Mapping The Journey

Where circles form on path well worn
The journeys separate
With chasing Wizard, running Dwarf
Each try to compensate

As Wizard takes road on the right
Dwarf goes the other way
Stays leftward on the map, in hope
Of living one more day

Chapter One
How It Came To be

I have a little tale to tell
It's written just for you
So once upon a time (I'll start
As all good stories do)

There was a little dwarf
And Perriwillow was his name
He often dreamed his fantasies
Of fortune and of fame

Of magic and of mystery
He liked to see them all
Fantasising danger
With all creatures great and small

He liked to whisper on the breeze
Conversing with the sun
A wild imagination
Always seemed to get things done

For in those days of far off lands
The sun would always shine
"Oh, how I wish," he hoped and dreamed
"A land like that were mine"

The other dwarves, they listened
But they didn't understand
He never could transport them
To his crazy, far-off land

Then one day, Perriwillow
He was walking on the shore
By the river, where it seemed to him
He'd live for evermore

And feeling sorry for himself
He felt like tender child
With magic running through his veins
Imagination wild

But then, he realised he was lost
The riverbank was strange
He'd wandered to a place which was
Outside 'Dwarf City's' range

"What can I do?" he cried aloud
"I'm all alone I fear
Am I to die all on my own?"
There was no-one to hear

The little dwarf began to sob
He crouched beneath the trees
"I wanted to live in a dream
But not such dreams as these

"I wanted worlds of fantasy
Adventures in them all
But all I've got is nightmares
Oh, I don't want this at all"

Then he heard a piercing voice
And tried to hide, in vain
"Behold, The Wicked Witch," she screeched
"And tell me – what's your name?"

"P-Perriwillow, Ma'am," said he
(He found it hard to speak
He hadn't got a thing to say
His legs had gone all weak)

"Well, Perriwillow, come with me
I've just the job for you
You'll be my slave and if you're bad
I'll cook you in my stew"

And so he had to follow
Pushed along by Witch's hand
Wherever would she take him
In this strange and hostile land?

Too soon, the dusk descended
And the darkness spread around
In the thickness of a forest
Full of strange and scary sound

"Now, go and find some firewood,"
She ordered Perriwillow
Then settled down, beneath a tree
The ground, her mossy pillow

At last the fire was all ablaze
And Dwarf he settled near
Until the Witch cried out to him
"You cannot sleep near here!

"The fire will not be your friend
You're not allowed to shirk
Go out into the damp and dark
It's not cold if you work"

So Perriwillow wandered round
To keep the cold at bay
And as the sun began to rise
He vowed, "I'll find a way

"I'll beat that Wicked Witch
She won't enslave me all my life"
Then silent, as all dwarves do move
He took his trusty knife

He moved toward the Wicked Witch
Revenge would end his plight
He had the figure, dressed in black
With tousled hair, in sight

"Oh, wretched woman," said the Dwarf
All set to use his blade
"If only you had been less mean
Good friends we could have made"

He raised his arm to strike the blow
Perfection in his aim
But from behind, he heard a voice
"I know your little game

"The real Witch is behind you
I'm not easy to defeat
You're lucky I don't kill you
Now, go find me things to eat"

So Perriwillow scuttled off
Thoughts rushing through his brain
To kill the Wicked Witch, it seemed
He'd have to try again

Finding food was quite a task
There wasn't much to find
Oh how he wished he had the food
He'd left so far behind

For back home, in 'Dwarf City'
There was always food to spare
Always quite enough for guests
Where people loved to share

But all that Perriwillow found
Were herbs and berries bright
Not a very welcome end
To such an awful night

He took them to the Wicked Witch
A frown upon his face
"Is this all you could find?" she cried
"You're really a disgrace"

"It's all that I could see," he said
And stared into the fire
"Well, get me some more firewood,"
She said, "you must not tire

"I told you, you will be my slave
With lots of work to do
You'll do my chores for all your life
There's no escape for you"

"That's what you think," he muttered
"Don't you take me for a clown"
He didn't know quite what to do
But yes, he'd bring her down

For whilst he was a prisoner
He'd be hungry, tired and cold
This wasn't how a Dwarf should live
For Dwarves were brave and bold

So Perriwillow made a plan
Of how to get things done
He'd help the Witch, she'd trust him
Then revenge, it would be won

He'd do the things she bid him
He'd stay through thick and thin
He'd be her trusty servant
She'd have no complaints of him

She'd think he wouldn't hurt her
As she slept, he'd plan the war
He'd use his wits, escape the Witch
And even up the score

So now the Dwarf returned to her
His arms were full of wood
Creating an illusion of
His efforts to be good

He'd have to work, to bide his time
He knew he'd find a way
To beat the nasty Wicked Witch
Take back his life, one day

"Well, my slave, you took your time,"
The Wicked Witch declared
"Did you try to run away
Then find you were too scared?"

"To run away, the thought had crossed
My mind," he said, "it's true
But as there's nowhere left to run
I came straight back to you

"I know that I was headstrong
When my fears got in the way
I'll try to be the best of slaves
I'm sorry, can I stay?"

"Well, I suppose so," said the Witch
"Amuse yourself nearby
And now, I'll check my lovely stew
To see if it's boiled dry"

The Dwarf could see it hadn't burned
She stirred with obvious glee
And Perriwillow thought, "I hope
That some of it's for me"

A long time since his breakfast
And although 'twas just one day
The smell of stew with berries
Simply took his breath away

"What are you doing?" asked the Witch
"Now, do yourself a favour
Sniffing at my stew - be gone
If life you want to savour

"Still, slaves can't be allowed to starve
So whilst I sit and eat
I'm giving you some berries
Now, go find yourself a seat"

Poor Perriwillow wandered off
With misery in his eyes
She wouldn't share her lovely stew
Though not a great surprise

For witches, (selfish, wicked ones)
Were never very kind
The Dwarf, he ate his meagre scraps
Tried not to lose his mind

He sank toward self-pity
Then descended, close to tears
When Witch cried out, in pain and rage
"Don't take my future years

"I'm much too young to die yet
But seems it's as I feared
Strong forces are against me"
- And with that, she disappeared

Perriwillow stared in awe
At where the Witch had been
Could not believe he'd witnessed
What his eyes had clearly seen

He looked into the steaming pot
No stew was left inside
The cauldron had upended and
The Witch had burned and died

In all her haste to eat the food
She'd been too mean to share
The pot had fallen to the ground
And stew splashed everywhere

It covered her, on arms and legs
Her head and body too
In scalding heat, she'd disappeared
As all dead witches do

Perriwillow cried, "I'm free
And free to find my way
Back to 'Dwarf City', go back home
Oh, what an awful day!"

But soon he spied a steaming bowl
Of herb and berry stew
The one the Witch was going to eat
A lovely smelling brew

"At least," he muttered, as he ate
"She left me this to eat
Before she went and spilt the rest
To cause her own defeat"

And so, he lay, amongst the trees
Allowed to sleep at last
His dreams filled with 'Dwarf City' lights
In shadows of his past

Chapter Two
The Awakening

When Perriwillow raised his head
From such a slumber deep
It had been many hours
Since he'd fallen sound asleep

What was it that had woken him?
He looked around to see
A group of several humans
Sitting underneath a tree

He tried to run and hide away
Then saw it was too late
He'd have to stay and face them
Then, no doubt would seal his fate

His knees, they knocked together
And his heart was full of dread
He couldn't face another awful day
And so, he said:

"I got lost on the riverbank
I'm really very tame
So please, do treat me kindly
Perriwillow is my name"

"Well, Perriwillow," said one man
"You're such a nice surprise"
The others, they just stared at him
Amusement in their eyes

"You think we want to hurt you?"
Said another "We're not hateful
You killed the Wicked Witch for us
We're really very grateful"

"You think I killed the wicked witch?
It really isn't true
She killed herself, I watched her,
Why, she killed herself with stew

"She bent to stir the mixture round
And in her greed and haste
She pulled the caldron from the fire
It really was a waste

"That stew was very tasty
With the herbs and berries bright
But most of it went over her
She must have died in fright

"And so, I didn't kill her
For I'm not so very brave
I only cared about myself
My skin I had to save"

"Oh, come now, Perriwillow," cried the men
"You mustn't tease
We know you killed the Wicked Witch
Now, tell your story, PLEASE"

The little dwarf, he realised that
They would not take his truth
For they believed in fairy tales
They'd heard back in their youth

They wanted to believe he was
A Hero, bright and bold
Brave and strong, the Conqueror
His story must be told

The men were sitting all around
Prepared with bated breath
To hear a detailed version of
The Wicked Witch's death

But no-one guessed the dwarf's reply
Just what he held in store
Said he, "The Wicked Witch is dead
Let's speak of her no more

"This is a time for merriment
And celebration long
It is a time for parties
And for wine and food and song

"Such stories are for later days
As you will clearly see
And now, because the Witch is dead
Let's wander wild and free"

The humans came from everywhere
Amongst the grass and trees
The sunlight followed them along
Their movement was the breeze

Now Perriwillow had been told
That humans were all bad
"It is not true," he laughed and sang
"Such good times to be had"

They laughed until the sky was dark
And stars lit up the night
Until firm friends were made by all
Their eyes and hearts alight

So one by one, they fell asleep
Each feeling it too soon
They wanted this fine night to last
In clear light of the moon

But as they slept and clouds did form
Things did not stay the same
Though peaceful slumber now was had
The evil forces came

They claimed the Witch's spirit
And they took it to her grave
Down in the murky depths below
Her evil tricks to save

You see, the Witch was not alone
Her friends would fly at night
To seek revenge upon the dwarf
They blamed him for her plight

At the dawn, the humans woke
From slumber sound, did rise
They knew not of an evil
Which was not meant for their eyes

Their breakfast was a merry meal
Of bread and cheese and meat
And Perriwillow felt content
The fire at his feet

But then, he had a sudden thought
He'd got nowhere to stay
He must make plans to travel home
Beginning right away

He stood up in the clearing
And he looked around in vain
He didn't know which way was home
And sat right down again

"Our little friend," a woman said
"You're frown is so revealing
You've many troubles on your mind
What is it that you're feeling?"

"A sense of loss, dear Madam,"
Said the dwarf, "It's very bad
I'm getting rather homesick
And I feel so very sad"

They asked him where he came from?
They asked if it was nice?
And did he want to go back home?
He cried, "At any price!

"I never meant to come here
And, although you're very charming
When I found out I'd wandered here
It really was alarming

"I used to dream so very much
Of people such as you
Adventures in strange places
Just as all young dreamers do

"But if you walked into your dreams
You'd feel the same as me
There's no place like 'Dwarf City'
For a dwarf to live, you see"

And then he sobbed, his head was bowed
Tears rolling down his cheeks
Said he, " I've been here two whole days
It feels like weeks and weeks"

The humans had no words to say
To dry his flowing tears
They could not help him get back home
They could not ease his fears

The witch had led him through the wood
They'd walked for half a day
Somewhere near here, the worlds collide
But could he find the way?

Through tiny paths she'd led him
Where she knew her way so well
But which route had she taken?
Perriwillow couldn't tell

There'd be no short cut for the dwarf
It really was a pity
Was there a path, so long and hard
To take him to 'Dwarf City'?

He must have got here in a spell
Created in a dream
In getting back, the dwarf had got
A problem, it would seem.

Then Perriwillow said aloud
"If I begin to roam
Along the bank that brought me here
It's sure to take me home"

"There is no river in these woods"
The oldest man replied
"Oh yes there is, I followed it!"
Young Perriwillow cried.

"'twas as I took my daily walk
Along the riverbank
That I left home, by accident
And my heart really sank"

"But little dwarf, we've told you
That there is no river near
It's your imagination
That such water brought you here"

Perriwillow trusted them
He did not feel deceived
It seemed there was no river
That's what all the men believed

"My friends, I do not doubt you
But I really haven't lied
It seems in coming to your world
That nature I defied

"There really was a river
But it seems, as I had feared
When it had safely brought me here
It promptly disappeared

"I know this sounds like fiction
But please don't think me rude
I need to ask for guidance
As my plans must be reviewed"

The dwarf continued with his speech
"I'll need some help from you
For instance, where am I to live?
Oh, what am I to do?"

"Now, don't you cry," the old man said
"We've heard all your confessions
And as you killed the Wicked Witch
You'll have all her possessions

"Including somewhere nice to live
A home through day and night
A place where you can sleep and work
A place so clean and bright

"Well, after we have tidied up
And painted it right through
The Witch left things in such as mess
It wouldn't do for you"

"Is it a cottage?" asked the dwarf
"A castle with a moat?"
"No," laughed the men, "you'll find it is
A long and narrow boat"

"A boat?" cried Perriwillow
As he scratched his stubbly beard
"There are no rivers near here
So I find that really weird

"Unless the boat is on dry land
It surely cannot be?
Or is it that – oh, tell me
Shall I live upon the sea?

"Or shall I live upon a lake
With waters clear and blue?"
They said, "Our boats are on canals
The Witch, she lived there too"

The dwarf looked very puzzled
His expression, it was grim
"Are there canals where you come from?"
The humans asked of him

"What are canals?" he asked the men
"'Dwarf City' it has none
We only have our rivers
And the sea to sail upon"

"Well, Perriwillow," said a man
"We have canals as well
And when at last you get back home
You'll have a tale to tell

"You'll tell of how our narrowboats
Are long and bright and gay
And how our simple life is lived
You'll love it more each day

"You'll tell them all about your boat
Enough to fill a book
But now, we have described enough
So come and take a look"

He followed them through tunnels
Made of trees, which lined the sky
He got so very tired
As he watched the miles go by

Then at last, the trees they cleared
The forest left behind
Perriwillow stared and stared
Emotion filled his mind

It really was a lovely sight
Which lay before his eyes
The water was so full of boats
With craft of every size

The oldest man, he led him
To the longest of them all
So low and black and narrow
Dwarfling tears began to fall

The sobs were tears of happiness
With no hint of self-pity
These strangers were as kind as folk
He'd left back in 'Dwarf City'

So Perriwillow dried his eyes
Without a hint of shame
And fondly, gazed at his new home
- 'Sarpedon' was her name.

Chapter Three
'Sarpedon'

Perriwillow stared, amazed
At what he had acquired
For things had happened very fast
He now felt very tired

His little legs were far too short
For walking all the way
To this fine place and now, he felt
He'd like to sleep all day

"Still," he thought, "'twas worth it
For this boat, she now is mine
A few small changes here and there
Will make her mighty fine"

The men knew what he needed
Now he'd finished his ordeal
The dwarf was very tired
And in need of a good meal

The women had prepared a feast
Of eggs and steak and bread
Perriwillow ate his fill
And afterwards he said:

"My friends, you seem to know when I
Am feeling at my worst
And if you showed me more concern
My heart would surely burst

"It's really very touching
Having friends who are so true
I hope that I'll be worthy of
Such noble folk as you"

"We're very sure you will," they cried
"No need to take a vote
And now you're fed and rested
Look inside you're lovely boat"

Perriwillow thought this seemed
A very good idea
His strength, it was returning
He was feeling in good cheer

He saw the hatch was open
So he went and peered inside
Everything was narrow
Not much more than six feet wide

The men, however, had been right
It wasn't hard to guess
That the Witch had not liked cleaning
For the boat was such a mess

Beyond the carnage left behind
A vision soon was planned
The dwarf would have things spick and span
With everything at hand

"It won't be very long," he said
"'till things look bright and new
I'll start to spring clean straight away
There's such a lot to do"

He started in the cabin
At the far end of the craft
So full of witches potions
"Oh, I must try these," he laughed

The bathroom, galley and saloon
Were pretty much the same
So full of coloured bottles
Which were painted with a name

All the names were different
And as far as he could tell
Each had a different potion
Made to cast a different spell

'Skin of Lizard', 'Slime of Toad'
He found and many more
Perriwillow picked them up
And threw them out the door

When at last he'd cleared them all
There was a pile so high
Outside the boat, upon the path
It reached toward the sky

Then calling to a passing man
"What can I do with these?
I can't use witches potions, so
Where can I put them, please?"

"We'll put them in the dustbin,"
Said the man, "I'll lead the way,
I'll show you where to take them
Though, it may not be today

"For first, we have to decorate
Let's wash and paint and clean
Let's make this boat the finest that
All worlds have ever seen"

And that's exactly what they did
It took them many hours
The boat was bright and clean
They even filled a vase with flowers

Again, the dusk was drawing near
'twas time to light a fire
To sit and eat and tell some tales
Before they must retire

They talked until their tales were told
And then they fell asleep
Each dreaming of their new-found hopes
Immersed in slumber deep

And in the morning, they awoke
To see the day so new
The man asked Perriwillow what
He'd really like to do

There were so many places where
The dwarf would like to go
"Please show me the canals," he said
"There's lots I want to know

"I still don't really know just what
They are, or where they lead
And as I'm going to live here, well
It's knowledge I will need"

"Oh, little Dwarf, you are so wise
And never think of fun
You always have to work and work
Until the job is done

"And now you want to learn about
Canals and all their ways
I'll teach you all I know
Though it will take us many days

"But first, we must have breakfast
I'll prepare a special treat,"
"Again?" thought Perriwillow
"All these humans do is eat"

So once again, the dwarf sat down
To yet another feast
He felt as though his skin had stretched
To twice its size at least

Bacon, eggs, then toast and jam
With cups of tea to follow
The dwarf, he ate so much, he felt
He'd not move 'till tomorrow

The man, he took it in his stride
He rose, prepared to go
"My friend, it's time we made a move,
Now, come on, don't be slow"

Perriwillow dragged his feet
Toward the waiting man
He said "Well, let's get started
Just as quickly as we can."

The dwarf was very quick to learn
His facts, he couldn't wait
He found canals were very long
And reasonably straight

With bridges that passed over them
And towpaths by the side
With hidden places, cold and dark
Where rats and mice could hide

Here, the country wasn't flat
The hills they rose and fell
And how canals climbed up and down
The man was going to tell

He told of how they opened gates
Then took the boat inside
You closed the gates and then
The water paddles opened wide

This strange device was called a lock
It helped you to descend
At other times it helped you climb
To destinations end

Canal life, it was very slow
Impossible to hurry
A life in hand with nature
Having very little worry

The man told Perriwillow
Of the many social places, called
Ale houses, which stood by canals
All full of smiling faces

"In one of these," he said "you'll see
How welcome you will feel
You'll sit down with a jug of ale
And eat a hearty meal"

And then, as if to demonstrate
That what he said was true
The man said "So, for lunch today
We'll go and find a few"

"It seems we're going to eat again,"
The little Dwarf despaired
"I think my skin is going to burst
I'm getting rather scared"

They set off down the towpath
Where an ale house they would find
Perriwillow felt quite ill
Now food was on his mind

For Perriwillow, all too soon
The ale house came in sight
Was it only lunchtime?
Would he live to see the night?

Two more meals to eat today
And both of human size
He felt quite sick, the thought of food
It swam before his eyes

And so, he mentioned to the man
That dwarves were only small
They couldn't eat as much as men
It did no good at all

It only made them fat and ill
They could not move with ease
Said Perriwillow, "So, could I
Have smaller portions please?"

The man, (his name was Terry), laughed
And said, "Of course, you're small
Dwarves should not eat the same as men
We're not the same at all"

And so, the Dwarf, he came to like
The ale house in the end
For Terry ordered one large meal
And a small one, for his friend

Far too many jugs of ale
Were kindly passed their way
With Perriwillow very pleased
They'd passed this way today

The ale, it made him merry
"But," said Terry, "Up you get
Let's find another ale house
Lunchtime isn't over yet"

The Dwarf, he wasn't used to ale
His legs felt awfully wrong
He wasn't walking very straight
That ale was very strong

He struggled down the towpath
Gently guided by the man
Who said, "Let's get a move on!"
Dwarf replied, "Not sure I can!"

Their progress it was slow, but soon
The ale house was in view
Another man appeared and said
"I need to speak to you

"The matter is quite urgent
And concerns the Witches death"
He paused his sentence for a while
To try and catch his breath

In a while, he spoke again
"The Witch had lots of friends
It seems that now they're seeking ways
To see that your life ends

"It is not safe to stay near here
It's best you move away
You need to go back to your boat
Prepare to leave today"

Perriwillow felt quite strange
In fact, he looked quite ill
Somehow he slurred an answer of
"I do believe I will

"I just don't want another fight
This time I might not win
I'll take my boat to stay alive
I never will give in"

So whilst the two men carried
Perriwillow home to bed
To sleep off all the ale he'd drunk
The second man he said:

"My name is Arnold, may I say
This is a serious game
I'll tell you all I know, but first
Please tell me, what's your name?"

"My name is Terry," said the first
"I'm Perriwillow's friend
Now tell me, what's this trouble
And a helping hand I'll lend?"

"The Wizard wants to catch the Dwarf,"
Said Arnold, "he's so sad
The Witch and he were closest friends
Revenge, it must be had

"They met when they were children
And their boats, together, moor
I dread to think just what he'll do
Or what he has in store

"And so, the Dwarf must leave here
As it isn't safe to stay
But after all the ale he's drunk
He'll not be moved today"

"Oh, yes he will," said Terry
"We can move whilst he's asleep
You see, I'm going with him
Through the darkness we will creep

"I'll face his danger with him
For it really is a pity
As all he ever dreams of
Is returning to 'Dwarf City'"

And so, the journey started
As they left, no tears were wept
And Perriwillow knew not
Of the danger, as he slept

Chapter Four
The Escape

When Perriwillow woke, at last
The dusk was getting deep
And though he had a headache
He felt better for his sleep

He stretched his limbs and rubbed his eyes
Then tumbled out of bed
The whole boat was vibrating
With the ache inside his head

"I won't do this again," he thought
"My head is very bad
It's hard to know how many jugs
Of ale I must have had

"I'll try and clear my head, I think
I'll stand outside my door
I'll walk around and get some air
For half an hour or more"

The splash, it was enormous
And the Dwarf got very wet
You see, he didn't know about
His latest journey, yet

He thought his mooring was outside
Its path all nice and dry
But now, he found the water
And he wanted to know why

Perriwillow shouted, "Help!"
And Terry stopped the boat
He thought it was hilarious
To see the Dwarf afloat

"It's strange to find you swimming
When you should be still in bed
I hope you've cured your headache now"
The man, still laughing, said

"What's going on?" the Dwarf replied
"We're out here in midstream
And as you know just where we are
You planned things it would seem?"

So Perriwillow slowly learned
That whilst he'd soundly slept
They'd glided from the Wizard's grasp
Escaping as they crept

It seemed the evil forces were
Abroad to do their best
To kill the Dwarf and get revenge
And so, he must head west

"'Dwarf City' lies toward the west
So westward we must roam,"
Exclaimed the Dwarf, with obvious glee
"I'm safe if I get home"

"My thoughts exactly," Terry said
"That's why due west we go
A journey of excitement
Or at least, I find it so"

The Dwarf, he wasn't quite so sure
His heart was full of fear
'twas he the Wizard hated
Was the end so very near?

"Enough now of this talking,"
Terry cried, "It's time we went
For you must learn to handle boats
You must be confident"

Perriwillow sighed aloud
Depressed with troubles new
At least his dip had cleared his head
But now what would he do?

The tears were forming in his eyes
His sobs about to start
When Terry cried, "The Wizard's here
Come on, we must depart"

The Dwarf jumped quickly to his feet
Escape was on his mind
He spied the Wizard, in his boat
So very close behind

He felt his knees begin to knock
In all his fear and strife
And then, with mighty roar
'Sarpedon's' engine revved with life

The shadows of the Wizard's eyes
Reflected deathly chill
As Terry cried, "To battle
For that fiend we aim to kill"

'Sarpedon' motioned quickly
Under Terry's expert hand
At this point, Perriwillow wished
He'd stayed upon dry land

He shouted out to Terry
"Now we'll never get away
The Wizard, he will capture us
We're sure to die today"

But Terry only smiled and laughed
'Sarpedon' stood her ground
She lay across the whole canal
In battle, onward bound

The Wizard cackled loudly
Now with victory in his eyes
He screeched, "I see, surrender
What a wonderful surprise"

He revved his engine, ready
For a short and powerful burst
To ram 'Sarpedon's' sides in
(Perriwillow feared the worst)

So, forward went the Wizard
With a grimace on his face
Game on, for if they blocked his path
He'd have to make a space

The impact, it was heavy
And it happened very fast
Perriwillow found it hard
To find something to grasp

He almost had to swim again
But managed not to fall
At least he'd save his dignity
If nothing else at all

The splintering was very loud
Which boat was going to win?
Then Perriwillow heard a splash
- The Wizard tumbled in

The Evil Boat was sinking fast
There really was no way
That Wizard would resume his chase
And catch the dwarf today

Terry had been right again
And Dwarf would have to learn
To trust the one who'd told him
There was no need for concern

The man had stood, so unperturbed
Throughout the Wizard's plight
He'd known from the beginning
Who was bound to win the fight

The Dwarf asked how he'd known
The Wizard's boat was going to sink?
Then added, "Oh, my headache's back
I had too much to drink"

"Well, you see, my little friend,"
The man began to speak
"The Wizard's boat is made of wood
And wood is fairly weak

"So when he tried to ram your boat
I had no fears to feel
He couldn't bring 'Sarpedon' down
Her hull is made of steel

"The Wizard did not stand a chance
He never could succeed
Which proves he didn't use his brain
To plan his evil deed"

They chuckled for a little while
But soon, they had to go
Continuing their journey
To an end they did not know

Then, at length, the friends discussed
The plans they'd have to make
To kill the Wizard, planning all
The moves they'd have to make

"It's time you learnt to handle boats,"
Said Terry, "You can steer
It's easy once you're taught the art
There's nothing bad to fear"

Perriwillow disbelieved
- It didn't look too easy
The thought that he'd be in control
Had made him feel quite queasy

He stood behind the engine
(That is where you need to be)
"Now watch the nose," said Terry
- Perriwillow couldn't see

The cabin, it was far too high
He couldn't see at all
This boat was built for men to steer
And dwarves were only small

"You'll have to stand upon this box
Before you try some more,"
Said Terry, "Now, go to the left,
You're heading for the shore"

The Dwarf, he pushed the tiller bar
And left he hoped to move
He didn't want to do this wrong
His friend would disapprove

He pushed it harder to the left
The bow began to show
That the boat was going anywhere
But where he meant to go

"My little friend," said Terry
"It's too late to start today
To steer 'Sarpedon' to the left
You push the other way

"It's much too dark to show you now
I shouldn't let you try
It's better in the morning light
When night has passed us by"

And so, they spent a peaceful night
With not too many cares
The Wizard's wrath was far away
Until he'd made repairs

All safely moored against the bank
Each dreamed his separate dream
Destruction of the Wizard was
A favourite, it would seem

The shadow of the dawn arrived
Before the friends awoke
They started off at once
This situation was no joke

Although, for now, the Wizard
In revenge could not pursue
He'd soon equip himself with boat
- So onward, journey new

The process was eventful
As 'Sarpedon' was untied
The Dwarf, he slipped and barely grabbed
The boat – oh, what a ride!

He said, "This life is hazardous
It's sure to make me old
If I get wet just one more time
I'm sure I'll die of cold"

Terry laughed, as Terry always did
Then said, "I'll 'drive'
Sit somewhere safe, you cannot drown
You have to stay alive

"Then later on, I'll teach you
How to steer your boat with ease
But now, you block my vision
Would you move a little, please?"

And so, their path continued on
With nothing much to say
The Dwarf relaxed and found he liked
To travel in this way

They moved along the straight canals
Then round each winding bend
And Perriwillow felt at ease
His nerves were on the mend

At last, they stopped for breakfast
Tied up closely to the side
The Dwarf felt very happy
With a smile he could not hide

Then Terry spoke, "It's time we moved
It's almost ten o'clock
And now, my friend, it's time for you
To pass through your first lock"

They slowly ventured further on
And nothing more was said
Until, in quiet solitude
The lock gates loomed ahead

Chapter Five
Lessons

'Sarpedon' glided to a halt
And just before the lock
Terry stepped off with the rope
As Dwarf looked up in shock

They'd passed beneath a gloomy bridge
Canal sides narrowed down
The lock gates looked almost as dark
As Perriwillow's frown.

"Will 'Sarpedon' fit in there?
It looks so very tight
And what on earth do we do next
To rise up to that height?"

"You start by getting off the boat,"
Said Terry, "Come on now
And grab the windlass, don't waste time
I'm going to show you how"

"What's a windlass?" asked the Dwarf
"I'm feeling rather slow"
"There's one upon the cabin top,"
Said Terry, "Off we go"

So Perriwillow grabbed the 'L shaped'
Handle in his hand
And carefully, he stepped ashore
To safety on dry land

He landed safe, he didn't trip
He felt that he could cope
But Perriwillow hadn't seen
The tied up mooring rope

His foot it caught and hard he fell
The concrete broke his fall
The mooring bollard missed his chin
Well, barely missed at all

No need to ask what Terry did
His laughter shed a tear
"What are you doing on the floor?
Get up, I need you here

"We've got no time to mess around
That Wizard is no joke
He'll soon be chasing us around
He's not a pleasant bloke"

And so, the Dwarf learnt very fast
The skills that he would need
Like any seasoned workboat crew
He'd work the locks at speed

"But safely," added Terry, "As
It really seems quite true
That you're rather prone to accidents
We know, you've had a few!

"Today, we'll concentrate on locks
Tomorrow, you can steer
So now, prepare your windlass arm
And let's get out of here"

Perriwillow wound the paddles
Happy as could be
Currents flowed beneath the gates
To set the water free

'Sarpedon' wriggled in the flow
Excited to move on
Straining at the (now obvious) rope
So anxious to be gone

Perriwillow pushed so hard
But gate, it was not ready
And then it gave, he grabbed the beam
To hold his street cred steady

These locks were only narrow, but
At bottom, had two gates
He had to open both of them
'twas one of his pet hates

Now some folk step across the gates
To save them walking round
But Terry said, "Your legs are short
Let's keep you safe and sound"

It really was quite sensible
Though maybe seemed unkind
And Dwarf would sometimes start to step
But always changed his mind

So you'd often see a running Dwarf
Who gradually got thinner
Could not afford to slow them down
But always wanted dinner!

Terry steered into the lock
Now empty, soon to climb
The running Dwarf shut both the gates
And paddles, record time

Then sprinting to the other end
And paddles winding open
Had time to watch and dream awhile
Where not a word was spoken

'Sarpedon' rose so gracefully
In all her ancient glory
Many a tale the 'Old Girl' had
But that's another story

Only one gate at the top
Two paddles still to close
Some people leave them open
But our Dwarf's not one of THOSE!

So off they went and on and on
Through every lock and mile
Heading north, to then head west
No time to stop awhile

They'd started out from Ashwood
And through Greensforge they did rise
The Navigation was the pub
Where ale did Dwarf surprise

But this time they were moving
As there was no time to dwell
No time to stop for food or drink
In fear of Wizards spell

Through Hinksford and through Swindon
Then through Wombourne they did climb
And now, as they approached 'The Bratch'
Another record time

"Always something new to learn,"
Said Terry, "Here you see
Three locks were built and then
Rebuilt, creating history

"Lots of people visit here
And history they are viewing
They watch the boat folk, 'specially those
Who don't know what they're doing"

Perriwillow said "Like me?
I know you swear and curse
I'm trying not to get it wrong
But fear I'm getting worse"

Terry smiled, "You're fine, my friend
Because you're being taught
It them that think they know
But never listen make me fraught!

"It's them that make it dangerous
And make the workboats slow
You're going to meet a lot of them
As on your journey go

"For times have changed and not all good
These days there's far more fuss
But let's get on, for we don't want
That Wizard catching us"

So, on they travelled, on and up
As miles and locks were eaten
Always in the knowledge that
The Wizard must be beaten

They didn't know just where he was
They didn't know his plan
But knew his evil forces
Would soon come, for Dwarf and Man

They didn't have an army
And defence, at best, was weak
But somehow, they would battle through
And answers they would seek

The day was getting shorter
Yet they felt it wouldn't end
So very weak and hungry, soon
Their needs they'd seek to tend

Perriwillow cried "Oh, look,
Here's Wightwick, see that sign?
'The Mermaid', we could stop and eat
I'm sure it would be fine"

"Too soon," said Terry, "Motor on,
It really is too early
We're not upon a pleasure cruise"
The Dwarf became quite surly

A few miles on, the same again
Through Compton they did glide
Perriwillow dared not moan
'The Oddfellows' he spied

"Aldersley Junction, just one mile,"
Said Terry, "Pay attention
To go the wrong way at this point
Is just too bad to mention"

It didn't take them very long
To reach where routes were parted
"Just keep 'Sarpedon' straight ahead
To get next section started"

Perriwillow breathed a sigh
Relief was surging through it
The other way was tight, he didn't
See how folk could do it

"To turn onto the '21'
To use the Local Name
It isn't hard if you know how
And exercise your brain

"'twas in the 1770's
An engineer, he came
And built the locks to climb the hill
James Brindley was his name

"The turn was built to be quite tight
And boatmen steered the way
They didn't need the practice
That folk often need today

"But very soon, my little friend,
You'll learn the skills you need
And as a boatman you become
On challenges you'll feed"

"How much further will we go
Today?" asked Perriwillow
"A few more locks, a few more miles
Then time for bed and pillow"

Said Terry, "Next, at Autherley
A toll house used to be
It's where we turn, for heading west
To where 'Dwarf City' be

"The Shropshire Union drops through lock
In legal terms revealing
That the old canal demanded this
Preventing water stealing"

The turning left, expertly done
By Terry, gave no grief
The shallow lock, no toll to pay
Somewhat of a relief

Then soon, a change of scenery
As banks were closing fast
Narrowing, at Pendeford
The Dwarf looked on, aghast

"However will we get through there?"
He heaved another sigh
"If someone comes the other way
How will we all get by?"

"There's lots of room," said Terry
"Though it's narrow, long and straight
For, like a layby, at the side
Are places you can wait"

So, underneath the motorway
Then countryside they meet
"Only a few more miles to go
Then something nice to eat

"Soon we will be mooring up
At somewhere nice and cheery,"
Said Terry, "And we've earned a pint
Our bodies, they be weary"

And so, they moored at Brewood
Got well settled for the night
The 'Bridge Inn' welcomed them inside,
With fire, burning bright

The pair enjoyed their steak filled pudding
Apple pie and cream
Washed down with ale, then off to sleep
Too tired, now, to dream

It's just as well they didn't know
That somewhere, far away
The Wizard's spells were ready now
To cast another day

Chapter Six
The First Plan

The Sun it rose and light it dawned
And travellers both awoke
The Wizard's wrath was foremost
In their minds, it was no joke

Refreshed from sleep and well aware
Of journey, now at hand
Confused where destination lay
As nothing, yet, was planned

They knew not of the Wizard's world
Or what he'd try to do
Where was it that he'd catch them up?
Their plans must start anew

"We'll talk as we are travelling,"
Said Terry, "Let's get going
We've lots of miles to do and
Of the danger there's no knowing

"Let's start off with the engine
As you need to know your boat
'Sarpedon' has a Lister
JP2, which has my vote

"I love the older engine
And it suits 'Sarpedon' well
Though it's not how she started out
Her story I will tell

"Built in 1936
Designed to carry load
A butty, paired with motorboat
'Sarpedon' would be towed

"But then she was converted
And her engine was installed
No longer working day and night
Domestic life it called

"So now she's independent
And can travel where you ask
Just treat her gently, with respect
She'll tackle any task"

The engine looked enormous
In the cabin, at the back
A war machine, the dwarf saw this
As first line of attack

The pipework ran from wall to wall
As far as he could see
Copper, brass and Lister green
It stood as tall as he

"Come back to earth," said Terry
"Check the oil, do you know why?
And gearbox, check the water too
If they run dry, she'll fry

"Take good care of her engine
And she'll always serve you well
Take note of all her moans and groans
And problems she will tell"

"How does it start?" asked Perriwillow
"Does it make you curse?"
"Lucky you, electric start,"
Said Terry, "Could be worse!"

The Dwarf, his head began to spin
With all it must retain
To understand and persevere
He'd have to 'up' his game

He stood upon 'Sarpedon's' stern
Determined as could be
He pushed her into gear and then
He listened carefully

She sounded like she'd try to stop
But Perriwillow knew
He had to wind the throttle on
And tell her what to do

"We'll make a boatman of you yet
It cannot be denied
But take it easy," Terry said,
"Too fast is suicide!"

The rope untied, 'Sarpedon' free
Three miles they had to go
To Wheaton Aston lock, then down
Descending with the flow

"Now don't forget," said Terry
"As we start to go downhill
Stay forward, near the bottom gates
Don't land upon the 'cill'

"The 'cill' supports the upper gate
Exposed as levels fall
If stern gets caught, a boat can sink
Not very good at all

"And if that isn't bad enough
Folk find out where you are
'Gongoozlers' love to see the mess
They come from near and far"

Soon they reached the open lock
Another boat came out
"Now that will speed our progress,"
Said the Dwarf, "Without a doubt"

He steered into the narrow space
Felt in control, at last
Then promptly banged into the wall
Said Terry, "Far too fast

"Now use reverse, you need to stop
'Sarpedon's' got no brake
Don't hit the gate, now rev her up
And NOW, for goodness sake!"

The heavy engine shuddered
As he gave her all he'd got
She stopped, just inches from the gate
The poor Dwarf's nerves were shot

"That'll teach you," said the man
"But no cause for concern
It takes a while to get it right
And still, you need to learn"

So safe descent completed
Wheaton Aston they departed
Now fourteen miles to Tyrely locks
The learning curve had started

Over little aqueducts
And Cowley, soon, they met
But Perriwillow didn't know
Where he was heading, yet

"It's time we started on a plan
Of what we're going to do,"
Said Terry, "How to get you home?
I haven't got a clue

"'Dwarf City' lies toward the west
It's true, but I confess
Just how we get from world to world
Is anybody's guess"

"Can no-one help us?" said the Dwarf
"This world is full of magic
There must be someone good, somewhere?
If not, it's rather tragic"

"I heard a rumour," said the man
"If we believe the tales
That we may find a Goodly Witch
In deepest, darkest Wales

"I really hope that this is true
Because, we need assistance
To beat the Wizard, find the path
Is going to take persistence

"I'm sure that she will seek us out
To keep us safe and whole
As magic forces we will meet
Beyond our own control

"For now, I guess we persevere
With journey long and slow
As dangers meet, our plans will change
Depending where we go"

So moving on, through Gnosall
And alongside Shelmore Wood
Then past a huge embankment
Just as quickly as they could

And soon, at Norbury junction
Where the Newport Branch once flowed
Down seventeen locks, where working boats
For years had carried load

But now, the path lies empty
With the use of just top lock
For maintenance of other boats
A covered, enclosed dock

Then next, to Grub Street Cutting
Where the 'High Bridge' towers tall
Carrying a busy road
But, what's that in the wall?

The bridge contains a second arc
To hold the bridge intact
"It looks so very scary,"
Said the Dwarf, "Evil in fact"

Said Terry, "Back in history
A telegraph pole, quite small
Carried wires, from point to point
So folk could make a call

"The pole, it has survived the years
As told in history book
No longer used, though still it stands
But evil it does look"

Perriwillow shuddered
Very glad that they were moving
He had a nasty feeling
With no sign of it improving

But as they passed beneath the bridge
The sparks began to rain
From high above, though no-one had
A clue from whence they came

And as the travellers looked above
Their fear, it grew and grew
For Wizard's face glowed in the arch
"Oh, what are we to do?"

Said Perriwillow, "We've been caught
And now we're going to die"
Terry yelled "Go faster
To escape, we have to try"

The booming voice, it echoed
In the bridgehole, as they passed
"I know where I can find you now
Your luck it will not last"

In wisps of smoke, the Wizard
Gone, as if he'd never been
Left Dwarf and Man, both questioning
Exactly what they'd seen

There was no choice of where they head
No point in turning back
Both hoping that there was a witch
To beat this maniac

So off to Wales, both fast and hard
And hoping to enlist
Good Witch's help, to find the door
Where worlds do co-exist

Though blinded to surroundings
In the rush to get ahead
They couldn't hide their darkened hearts
So full of fear and dread

The Dwarf saw little of his trek
Past village, pub and land
Where would he find the courage that
The Wizard would demand?

The day was long, the miles went by
And Tyrely locks went down
Then wooded stretch, well roofed by trees
To Market Drayton town

"How long to go before we stop?"
Poor Perriwillow asked
"What else to fear by end of day
With Wizard's wrath, unmasked?"

"Just six more miles," said Terry
"But I think it's clear to see
That the quicker we can find some help
The happier we'll be

"I know today is very long
But look how far we've travelled
Plus, things we'd wish we could forget
As plans we have unravelled

"But still, there is a way to go
To put us to the test
Two flights of locks will take us down
Before we get some rest"

At Adderley, they did arrive
And five locks down did work
The dusk it fell and both did fear
Where evil forces lurk

But soon, the sight of Audlem locks
Did stretch, descending long
The Dwarf said "Oh, I can't go on"
The Man said "Just stay strong

"Just look ahead, at lighted wharf
And building full of cheer
Of comfort, food, the rest we need
To wake with head that's clear

"The landlord is a friend of mine
I never pass him by
Protection, he will offer us
Inside the 'Shroppie Fly'"

Chapter Seven
The Barricade

The 'Shroppie Fly' was warm and safe
As travellers, weary, rested
Their courage, here, they would renew
For nerves would soon be tested

The landlord, Arthur, sat them down
Where no-one else would see
They talked, the plans they grew
To set poor Perriwillow free

What started as a quiet dream
Was now a dark nightmare
The Dwarf could not help thinking
That he wished he was elsewhere

But here he was and what came next
Was somehow down to fate
So leave they must and very soon
The Witch they must locate

"Eight miles to go and five locks down
Toward Wales, your truth to learn
Through Nantwich, then at Hurleston,"
Said Terry, "Left we turn"

And so, they did begin the trek
As planned, it started well
Made good time, locks kept heading down
The levels slowly fell

Then at the very lowest point
And onward, north, still go
'till over iron aqueduct
To where, they could not know

On reaching Nantwich Basin
Where the channel, wider grows
As old canal, it joins the new
And water meets and flows

Next, the banks they curve and bend
Where hearts much faster beat
As junction spied, where into Wales
They'll go, the Witch to greet

"There seems to be a lot of boats,"
Said Terry, "Hold her still"
But what they saw was not good news
Their luck had gone downhill

Perriwillow stopped the boat
He'd never felt so scared
The man, he too, was terrified
A fear they both now shared

Though junction went toward the left
A boat had blocked the way
It seemed there would be little chance
Of heading west, today

It seemed unlikely, at this time
That death would be delayed
The odds were stacked against them
As they faced the barricade

"I'll have you now," the Wizard cried
"There's no way to escape"
He smiled the smile of evil men
His plan was taking shape

"I've blocked the lock; you can't get past
And help you will not find
You can't get to the gateway
Where the worlds become aligned

"I will not have your mischief
For you killed my oldest friend
Be sure that I will get revenge
On that, you can depend"

He stood atop the lock gates
As a chanted spell did cry
His arms extended, face upturned
Wand pointed to the sky

"Spirits where the waters meet
I call upon your aid
To curse the Dwarf, who killed my friend
And let the debt be paid"

The heavens darkened; thunder rolled
Then lightning filled the sky
The chill was felt across the land
As evil floated by

Perriwillow shivered hard
Awaiting of his fate
The Wizard looked just awesome
As he towered above the gate

Powerful and timeless
As the stuff of nightmares grew
"Well, if you think I'm beaten," cried the Dwarf
"Then join the queue!

"There's plenty things much worse than you
Like how I'm getting home
I didn't kill your friend, so there!
Now just leave me alone"

The Wizard's face turned ashen grey
In anger and confusion
The way this Dwarf had challenged him
Was surely an illusion?

He shook his fists, in anger true
His temper broke the spell
The Wizard moved along the gates
- Stepped off the edge and fell

He landed soon and very hard
Upon his startled crew
Aboard his boat, beneath the lock
His street cred, now askew

The Motley Mob had scattered
So they hardly broke his fall
The Wizard said "You useless lot
You're just no good at all"

"But Wally," said a scrawny man
"That's really quite unfair"
"My name is 'WALTER'," Wizard said
"Can't take you anywhere"

Terry started laughing
As it seemed almost untrue
The Wizard's luck had turned and now
He'd met his 'Waterloo'

The Tyrant, he had filled their world
With major fear and dread
Still, Terry couldn't understand
Inside the Wizard's head

A tiny 'plastic cruiser'
Carried Wizard and his mob
Said Terry, "You'd have thought
He'd pick a boat up to the job"

"It's not my fault," the Wizard spat
"It's all that I could get
You sank my lovely, wooden home
For that, I'm still upset

"Don't think that this is over
And you treat me like a clown
I tell you, I'm not having it
That Dwarf, I'm bringing down

"You still can't get into the lock
To Wales you cannot go
I've many friends to help me now
You're end you soon will know"

"Terry, oh, what shall we do?"
Poor Perriwillow stuttered
"It seems I won't be getting home
If evil spells are muttered"

The Motley Crew had pulled themselves
Together, standing strong
The tiny boat still blocked the way
The Dwarf's plan, gone so wrong

The Wizard raised his arms and wand
Preparing spell to cast
But unexpected turn of fate
Made everyone aghast

A throbbing sound, a battle roar
As from the north appeared
A mighty coalboat, working hard
Into the junction steered

'Mountbatten' bore down on the space
The 'plastic boat' was blocking
For those who watched, there was no doubt
That impact would be shocking

The crew jumped, like deserting rats
The Wizard still stood firm
His wand held high, to chant a spell
Would 'Wally'' never learn?

'Mountbatten' hit the little boat
And caused resounding crack
The fibreglass, it buckled
Under steel – no turning back

"Get out the way," yelled Richard
"Have you nothing else to do?
We're trying to work, now shift, we've got
No time to mess with you"

Walter tried to hold his stance
Collapsed as boat went down
His wand still raised above his head
Afeared that he would drown

If he had hit the water, then
It wouldn't have hurt so badly
He landed on 'Mountbatten's' bow
His arm still waving madly

"I curse you all," said Walter
"And my spells will do their worst"
Ruth, Richard's wife, ran up the boards
"Not if I curse you first

"Don't you threaten me, you Fiend
And let me make it clear
I don't know who you think you are
Your games won't work round here

"I'll tell you once, now, off my boat
It's time you took a swim!"
She hit him with the 'buckby can'
And knocked the Wizard in

Wally thrashed around a bit
His dignity to keep
"If you can't swim, stand up," said Ruth
"It's only four feet deep"

The Motley Crew, they fished him out
And tried to get him dry
It hadn't been the day they'd planned
Which no-one could deny

"Now get that wreck out of our way,"
Said Richard, "No more shirking
We don't need amateurs like you
To stop us in our working

"Oi, Perriwillow, don't go north
The Wizard's mates are waiting
So get turned round and head back south
No need for hesitating"

The look of shock shown by the Dwarf
Made Terry feel quite sad
Who knew where Dwarf would need to go?
What chance of home he had?

"I'll turn her round," Said Terry, "Now,
It's time for us to move
It's pretty tight, with 'by-wash' flow
But luck's due to improve"

The turn was uneventful
And they soon were on their way
With Wizard's boat disabled
It would keep the Fiend at bay

Ruth and Richard waved them off
With no good news to share
Perriwillow shed a tear
No comfort anywhere

"No time for moping," Terry said,
"Now back from whence we came
If Witch exists, she'll seek us out
And help us with our aim"

They headed back to Audlem and
With heavy hearts they travelled
But magic forces filled the air
As newer threads unravelled

A Lady stood above the lock
And watched the workboats go
A windlass in her tiny hand
Her voice so calm and low

"Hello Wally, how are you?
I see you're bright as ever
Using brains is not you're thing
You've never been that clever"

"Hello Stella," he replied
"I'll get that Dwarf, don't fear
No sympathy he'll get from me
He is not welcome here"

She walked away and stood awhile
Her thoughts were hers, alone
The little Dwarf was innocent
Just wanted to get home

Though Stella Bella hated fools
Her heart gave others light
With hippy clothes and dreadlocked hair
Her character was bright

She raised her windlass, softly spoke
With words as hard as nails
Her spell, to keep the Dwarfling safe
- The Goodly Witch from Wales

Chapter Eight
The Counsel

The 'Shroppie Fly', still welcoming
Though truth was slowly dawning
This trip would be a tricky one
With dangers and no warning

Arthur flagged 'Sarpedon' down
And signalled Dwarf to moor
In quietest place along the wharf
They quickly stepped ashore

Much planning now would be required
And counsel they must seek
They couldn't do this all alone
With future looking bleak

"We have to cover up the boat,"
Said Arthur, "She must hide
And when 'Sarpedon's' tucked away
We'll all meet up inside"

They laid tarpaulins over her
And camouflaged her well
The Wizard, now, was in pursuit
Well-armed through magic spell

"Now quickly, get inside the Inn
As there, you can lie low
Where friends you'll meet and help receive
To plan where next you go"

Terry took a final look
To check that boat was hidden
Perriwillow went inside
To do what he'd been bidden

Seats inside had been reserved
In corner, dark and warm
Where hidden, safe from prying eyes
Some new ideas were born

Perriwillow didn't know
The folk around the table
But all were sharing great concern
To do what they were able

It seemed the Wizard was well known
For antics far and near
Caused havoc everywhere he went
And spread a web of fear

They all agreed he must be stopped
His wrath was everywhere
But mostly trying to catch the Dwarf
Which wasn't very fair

The saving grace, they did agree
He wasn't very good
At anything he tried to do
So beat the Fiend, they would

Perriwillow said, "It's clear
He's never, ever sorry
I know his name is Walter, but,
He really is a Wally"

Laughter rippled round the room
From those around the table
And all would do their level best
To keep the Wizard stable

They pooled their information
And there really was no doubt
That Walter was in hot pursuit
To seek 'Sarpedon' out

Their sources said he'd found a boat
And heading south was bound
But yet again, his plans gone wrong
He'd run the boat aground

"It hasn't stopped him," said a man
"They soon were on their way
And Wally's vowed to catch you up
Before the end of day"

Perriwillow turned quite white
With thought of being captured
If someone recognised his boat
Their cover would be fractured

Just as his fear began to grow
They heard a mighty crash
A lot of shouting, followed by
Inevitable splash

Arthur went outside to see
What carnage he could find
A hire boat, large, out of control
It's path all misaligned

The Wizard stood upon the stern
With tiller in his hand
A woman cried "Who let him steer?
He really should be banned"

The counsel peered through open door
Afeared of what they'd see
Relief, 'twas only Wally
Steering boat through bankside tree

It's true, he'd hit 'Sarpedon'
But he didn't realise
All covered in tarpaulins
Hadn't seen through her disguise

The Dwarf could not believe his luck
They hadn't got a clue
One dripping crewman, running hard
The hire boat motored through

'Sarpedon' was undamaged, well
Wally had almost missed
The hire boat kissed her slender hull
In ghostly, evil tryst

The Counsel, they had reconvened
Now firmly in belief
That Walter had now run ahead
Somewhat of a relief

"Let's get this meeting back on track,"
Said Terry, "Let's move on
From what I hear, we need to take
The dreaded '21'"

"The grapevine tells that fate is kind
To make us less frustrated
The Witch has moved, we'll find her in
Stoke Bruerne, she's relocated

"Beneath the bottom lock she lives
Our plight we can explain
The Goodly Witch will help us
'Stella Bella' is her name

"So back we go, from whence we came
Then into climbing flight
To Wolverhampton, Birmingham,
Then south, to put things right

"The Wizard is in front of us
But in pursuit he's racing
He wrongly thinks we're well ahead
And so, he will keep chasing

"That gives us space to talk awhile
Of things we need to do
To eat and drink and get some sleep
To find who'll help us through"

They talked of plans, supplies to take
Like water, fuel and food
They needed to be well prepared
The Counsel did conclude

They talked of names, of whom to seek
To help them on their way
The working boats and friends of theirs
Would see them through each day

"It isn't right," the Dwarf exclaimed
"To find I have been blamed
For what I clearly didn't do
The Wizard should be shamed

"We could have talked this problem through
Discussed his fear and doubt
But seems he's just a nasty man
I'm better off without"

"He's not much of a Wizard though,"
An old man softly spoke
"His Crew, they take the 'micky'
And they treat him as a joke

"But still, you must be careful
You must hold him in your sight
For on the odd occasion
Walter gets the magic right

"And then, he's mean and ruthless
For his evil is empowered
His temper, vented on his Crew
A bully and a coward"

"Well bullies always meet their match,"
Said Terry, "His began
At Hurleston, when that woman
Hit him with her 'buckby can'"

The Counsel laughed, at thought of Ruth
As 'buckby can' did hurl
Old Wally's ego soon went down
When clouted by a girl

"With talk of coalboats," Arthur said
"Their network is quite strong
They feel your pain about your plight
And think the Wizard wrong

"The workboat folk are family
Though community now small
Their moral codes are tough
So upset one, upset them all

"You'll hear of where the Wizard moves
Though not that hard to track
For Wally's wayward ways ensure
He's never welcomed back

"So on that note, get rest and sleep
For sun it soon will rise
Another day to journey on
And fast if you are wise

"Await your help, for it will come
You do not go alone
Your plans will change along the way
When troubles rise, unknown"

And that's exactly what they did
They slept a peaceful night
Bid farewell to the 'Shroppie Fly'
On morning clear and bright

With tracing of their downward steps
Now upwards they did climb
Through Adderley, Market Drayton town
And Tyrley, record time

They barely ate, they barely slept
Just journey on their mind
Awaiting news from working crews
Their lives now intertwined

Through Shebdon, going miles and miles
No locks to slow them down
At High Bridge, feared the sparks would fly
No sign of Wizard frown

Past Norbury, covered mile on mile
Their course so straight and true
Did not expect to be back here
Plans didn't feel so new

And then, through Wheaton Aston lock
Past Brewood, journey kind
Then finally, back to Autherley
Where stop lock leave behind

Perriwillow felt quite good
Despite the serious goal
His steering hadn't half improved
He now felt in control

They left the Shropshire Union
For the Staffs and Worcester, south
Then heading for the '21'
At Aldersley Junction mouth

Perriwillow motored on
As yet, he had no knowing
Why Terry shouted, very loud
"Be careful where you're going!"

Perriwillow screamed in shock
At what it was he saw
Fast moving boat was pushing waves
And Dwarf looked on in awe

It had to be the Wizard
And impending cataclysm
Heavy engine, Bolinder
A strange, uneven rhythm

"Hold your line," bawled Terry,
"Don't you waver by an inch
It's 'Greyhound', 'Captain Cargo'
Keep your street cred, don't you flinch!"

The boat approached and closer
Bearing down and loaded low
Perriwillow swallowed hard
The boat appeared to slow

Just marginally, you understand
And just enough to shout
"Don't go up on the '21'
Some fool has wiped it out!"

The steerer wound the throttle on
And stern dug deep through water
As Greyhound disappeared from view
There's few who could have caught her

"That was Malcolm," Terry said
"A message mailed in style
It sounds like Wally strikes again"
He added, with a smile

And so it was, the plan it changed
Again, where waters parted
To Ashwood, backtrack, all the way
To where the journey started

Chapter Nine
What Walter Did

When Walter passed the 'Shroppie Fly'
He was incensed with rage
How dare the Dwarf belittle him
To take the centre stage

Walter didn't like to lose
Expected not to fall
He thought he ruled the world and yet
Had nothing much at all

They'd sunk his home and made him swim
His life was upside down
And when he finally caught the Dwarf
He'd really go to town

He'd make him suffer, yes, he would
Of that there was no doubt
He sat inside the hired boat
No point in going out

He shouted at his Mottley Crew
Made them do all the work
And every time they got it wrong
He'd sulk and go berserk

Yes, Wally was a charmer
Who knows why each man stayed?
I guess it gave them quite a laugh
When Wizard got dismayed

Their journey was eventful
As a lot of things they'd hit
'Sarpedon' was the first of them
Not recognised a bit

The Mottley Crew, to give them due
They never seemed to falter
They weren't too good at handling boats
But far advanced on Walter

No-one guessed 'Sarpedon' stopped
As Bernard had directed
So half a day and gaining on
Dwarf progress they expected

I'm sure that if they knew the truth
They wouldn't push so hard
But Wally never listened and
Advice would disregard

A chip upon his shoulder sat
And always knowing best
Forever someone else's fault
For failure in each quest

Folk told them that they hadn't seen
'Sarpedon' moving through
"You're trying to trick me," Wally said
"I won't take heed of you!"

They bashed and bawled their way along
As fast as boat would go
Believing through each manic mile
They'd catch the Wizard's Foe

For them, the damage wasn't bad
Just little bumps and scratches
For Walter, inside, sulking hard
Had battened down the hatches

They took the self-same journey
That our Dwarf would reach, in time
And when they reached the '21'
They entered, starting climb

A Brindley project, as we know
With engineering true
From Aldersley to Birmingham
To speed the cargoes through

Though started off as twenty locks
Lock twenty proved too deep
So added more, now twenty-one
Stopped water use too steep

Canal was built to transport coal
As roads were poor and slow
A narrow route around the land
To keep the costing low

Flight rose, it climbed through narrow locks
With much hard work required
The summit high, so no surprise
Successful crews got tired

An average crew will four hours take
Or three, if make good speed
But how long would the Mottley Crew
To reach the top lock need?

If journey weren't so serious
Amusement could be found
In watching Wally and his Mob
Avoiding getting drowned

They started up, the lock was in
Their favour, open gate
More time be gained if easy climb
Through flight, a twist of fate

The second lock (lock twenty, now)
Inserted, last of flight
Just one gate built at either end
Would Wally get it right?

The dullest of the Mottley Crew
Had gone ahead to set it
The rest of them had set him up
They knew he wouldn't get it

Their laughter rang aloud with mirth
At crewman's great expense
Explaining of the single gate
With laughter, did commence

The side hatch of the boat thrown wide
And Walter's head appeared
"What's going on, you useless lot
Get on with it," he jeered

With that, he disappeared from view
And slammed the hatches shut
One day he'd slam so hard that they
Would fall into the 'cut'

They carried on, past racecourse
Slowly climbing, paddles winding
More rural, Oxley viaduct
With history in the finding

The Crew became quite interested
In things to see and do
The Science Park, the Gas Works
Where, in 1862

Balloon had launched, world record set
No oxygen used in rising
Stour Valley, 22 arches built
Historically surprising

The Ceres Works, then Fowlers Park
Where railway lines converged
Canal diverted, sharpened bend
Where new rail line emerged

The Mottley Lot became engrossed
In what they did not know
They hadn't seen a lot of school
They never used to go

They even started chatting
Sounding much like 'normal' folk
'till banging side hatch brought them back
And vicious Wizard spoke

"Well this is nice, my little Crew
I'm pleased you're having fun
I don't suppose you've found the Dwarf
To have this journey done?"

"We're nearly at the top," said one
"Just three more locks to do
We'd go a little faster if
We had some help from you"

The Wizard didn't like that
For he had to be in charge
No good at anything he did
But still, he gave it large

He puffed his chest, as if in rage
But then appeared to stall
For if he couldn't win the fight
He said nothing at all

He ducked inside the hired boat
With characteristic sneer
Appearing, back upon the stern
Intending now to steer

Lock number three was ready
And the poor boat lurched ahead
But Wally wasn't accurate
The 'cill', it stopped him dead

Boat bounced back from the impact
And the Crew suppressed a smile
As Wally took the lock in his
Inimitable style

The Crew became efficient
Thus avoiding further wrath
Annoying Wizard further could
Result in bankside bath

So up they rose and safely
As the paddles they did wind
To raise the boat and motor on
Now leave the lock behind

Just two more locks to reach the top
Of flight, not long to wait
For number two was straight ahead
No luck with open gate

Now Wally had to try and stop
Selected hard reverse
He managed, just, to pull her up
With use of swear and curse

The Mottley Crew let water out
Reducing level, fast
Impatient Wizard, edging in
With water gushing past

"The gates aren't ready," someone said
"You'll have to wait awhile"
"Don't try and tell me what to do,"
Said Wally, full of guile

"I've seen those nasty working boats,"
He said, "They push them open
They hold their boats upon the gates
And not a word is spoken

"They never do them damage
So their ways I won't condemn
Now I will push the gates today
I'm just as good as them"

The chorus came "Don't do it!"
For his boating skills were awful
The damage would be massive
Not to mention, here, unlawful

So, wilfully he rammed the gates
Full throttle, barging through
The Mottley Crew, they shouted "STOP"
But not much they could do

The splintering gates resisted
Well, that was, until they gave
One gate hung off its hinges now
Impossible to save

"That's got us in," said Wally,
"See, I told you I could do it"
He didn't even realise
The fact he'd gone straight through it

There was an eerie silence
As, except for sound of water
The Crew could sense their worsening fate
Like lambs led to the slaughter

One gate was lying, half-way off
It's hinges hanging loose
With no way now to make the climb
Through Wally's gross misuse

"Just look at what you fools have done
Now fix it!" came the yell
One Mottley Crew, sarcastic, said
"Why don't you cast a spell?"

The Wizard raised his evil wand
As if the man to curse
Then pointed at the broken gate
Said Crew, "This will get worse"

The air it cracked; the water swirled
The men stepped back in shock
The gate fell off its broken hinge
And crashed into the lock

The boat was now completely trapped
With gate across her stern
No way that they could run away
Go up, go back, or turn

A crowd had formed around the lock
Excited by the action
News travelled quick, along canal
And spread the satisfaction

"Oi, Wally," said an onlooker
"You've sunk another boat
The weight of gate has pushed her down
No way that she can float"

"My name is 'WALTER'," came the shout
In tantrum, giving large
"I don't care what your name is,"
Said a voice, "Are you in charge?"

"I am indeed," the Wizard crowed
"Who am I speaking to?"
"I'm Ray, 'Canal Authorities'
I need to speak to you"

"Just get this fixed so we can go
Your lock had faulty gate
And when it fell, it sank my boat
I hope you compensate!"

The stifled laugh belonged to Ray
But also Mottley Crew
Plus Gongoozlers and Boaters
Who'd arrived to join the queue

"We'll have to get this mess cleaned up,"
Said Ray, "Don't make this hard
Accept that it was all your fault
You won't come out unscarred"

And then, as if to prove a point
A man from boat, now waiting
Waved windlass at the Wizard's head
No hint of hesitating

"You'll cost us several days," he said
"Our load will be delayed
It's you what owes for loss of time
If compensation's paid"

"So get this done," our Wally cried
We need to get away
"It won't be fixed 'till Monday now,"
Said Ray, "It's Saturday

"I'll call upon what callout crew
We've got, we're understaffed
And call the Hire Boat company
Tell them you've sunk their craft"

So Walter spent the weekend
Giving statements of his plight
He didn't see much sympathy
And tantrums ruled the night

He swore and cursed the time away
Behaviour so unkind
As 'Sarpedon' took another route
Thus, leaving them behind

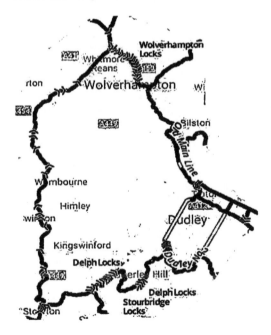

Chapter Ten
Begin Again

The winding, long and lonely road
To Ashwood slowly led
Perriwillow didn't like
The thoughts inside his head

He felt depressed, he couldn't eat
His plans had come undone
The Dwarf was quite exhausted
But for him, sleep wouldn't come

They'd travelled hard and made their plans
But journey, now prolonged
There seemed no way of getting home
And back where he belonged

He tried to turn his thoughts around
To think of plans anew
It's not as if he had a choice
He had to see things through

Terry steered 'Sarpedon'
Every mile felt long and slow
Perriwillow worked the locks
Where next? He didn't know

He didn't see the sense of it
For who could lead the way?
No guarantee that Witch would know
Just where 'Dwarf City' lay

"That's if, indeed, we find the Witch,"
The Dwarf suppressed a moan
"On every route we take, the Wizard
Stops me getting home"

Terry didn't disagree
As journey did recall
It seemed they'd travelled day and night
To go nowhere at all

But still, this thinking didn't help
And onward they must move
Right back to where they started from
In hope luck would improve

The journey was a heartless blur
The Dwarf was lost in thought
When Terry said "We're nearly 'home'
So don't get too distraught

"We're at 'The Navigation', where
I'm going to ask for news
The Wizard may be waiting
So we have to look for clues

"His mooring, it is next to yours
And though he isn't near
He may have friends who lie in wait
They will not want you here"

The landlord he supplied some food
Refreshing weary pair
Each knowing that the dangers grew
And all must stay aware

'The Navigation' was like home
And travellers felt dismay
They could not dare to stop awhile
Though both would like to stay

Their Fiendish Foe would soon find out
If long they stayed in here
For soon, the Wizard's friends would come
To take their fill of beer

So sadly and reluctantly
The Dwarf and Terry went
With only hope and courage left
To ease their discontent

'Sarpedon', she was waiting
Not a single word was said
As lock was drained and boat descend
All keen to get ahead

On leaving Greensforge, silent still
Ashwood Marina spy
Where Wizard's Mob, enjoying ale
Missed Dwarf and Man go by

From here, canal becomes remote
See rooms carved in the rock
And very soon, again descend
At pretty Rocky Lock

Now at the bottom, Terry steered
Toward the open flow
When Perriwillow, turning white, called
"Quick, we've got to go!"

"What's wrong," said Terry, looking up
"You're in a state of panic"
Dwarf cried "The Wizard's mates are here
And looking pretty manic"

Perriwillow looked behind
Where cycling hard and fast
From down the towpath came the Mob
As Dwarf looked on, aghast

"Jump on," cried Terry, "Quickly now,
We can't afford to wait
Though not quite sure what we can do
Our chances aren't that great"

Perriwillow jumped aboard
In fact, he almost dived
He landed on the cabin top
In awe that he'd survived

The shouting, getting louder
From behind, as Angry Horde
Now getting far, far closer
Than 'Sarpedon' could afford

"They're chasing us on cycles,"
Said the Dwarf, "We can't escape"
Said Terry, "Don't give up, but yes,
We're really in a scrape"

The pair looked back above the lock
To where the Tribe was huddled
Discussing of a fateful plan
Which soon became quite muddled

Then without warning, on his bike
A Scrawny Fiend rode on
Toward the chasm, under lock
The boat to land upon

But this was one of Wally's crew
Not chosen to be clever
As Terry, he supressed a smile
At cyclist's next endeavour

Put in reverse, 'Sarpedon' stopped
As cyclist, in mid air
Still pedalling hard to reach the boat
Which simply, wasn't there

He landed with a mighty splash
Beyond 'Sarpedon's' bow
The Wizard's mates were laughing loud
Not much threat from them now

Terry didn't hang around
Like any working boater
He wound 'Sarpedon's' engine up
And left the flailing floater

Arms and legs thrashed everywhere
As cyclist lost his pride
"Why don't you just stand up, you fool"
Our Perriwillow cried

"Shift yourself," said Terry
"Have your senses gone astray?
If my propeller carves you up
You'll wish you'd stayed away"

"Who do you think you're talking to?"
Another Twit retorted
"You can't say that, you're being rude
I'll have your boat reported"

"Just go ahead," the Dwarf said
"But, perhaps you should rethink?
It's not our Crew that took a bike
And threw it in the drink"

He added, "Wally won't be pleased
About this bit of fun!
And don't forget to shut the gate
Behind you, when you're done"

When Perriwillow looked behind
He heard a mighty din
The Mob were trying to find the bike
But kept on falling in

For now, 'Sarpedon' could move on
With Wally's threats unfounded
But it was clear that soon he would
Be back, with wrath unbounded

The Dwarf must push through miles ahead
For Wizard would be told
Of where 'Sarpedon' travelled now
As journey did unfold

Terry knew the route they planned
His fears remained unsaid
They'd need to take another path
Just two more miles ahead

He hoped the way was open
And without a barricade
More detours they could do without
No wish to be delayed

Through Gothersley they carried on
In lock, no trouble met
Past Devils Den, where boathouse cut
In rock, no problems yet

Around the bend and heading now
For Stourton, so afraid
With Terry getting more disturbed
In fear of a blockade

On turning left, they saw the locks
A tiny flight of four
Canal was clear to Stourbridge, here
No conflict was in store

Terry sighed and breathed relief
"Let's hope our way stays clear
The Wizard's on the other road
And should not come down here

"News tells he wrecked the '21'
'twas him, as we had guessed
He's stuck there for a little while
For that, I feel we're blessed

"But now, we take the longer road
Have faith your luck will hold
We need to get to Birmingham
Ahead of Wizard bold

"It is a hard and winding path
The locks will seem unending
A journey steeped in history
But courage may need mending"

So on and up they started and
The four locks soon were eaten
Enthusiasm, now renewed
Refusing to be beaten

A brief respite, to take a breath
Though checking watch for time
Past junction, choice for Stourbridge Arm
But now, a longer climb

Up sixteen locks they had to go
Approached as darkness fell
"I can't go on," the Dwarf cried out
"I'm feeling quite unwell"

"We cannot stop," said Terry
"Still we have a long commute
If we don't reach the Mainline first
That Fiend will block our route"

So up the flight, through Glasshouse Bridge
And past the Redhouse Cone
Where Stuart Crystal Glass Works stood
And handmade glass was blown

Past Dadfords shed, the strangest lock
Round Brierley Hill, path bends
Delph Bottom Lock comes into sight
And Stourbridge Canal ends

Perriwillow saw the rise
Of next flight, climbing high
Resigned to yet more hours of toil
Beneath the darkened sky

But through one lock and Terry said
"I think it's time we rested
We need to gather strength anew
For courage will be tested"

They moored on wharf, above the lock
Where workboats used to pause
And for a short while, slept
Before resuming of their cause

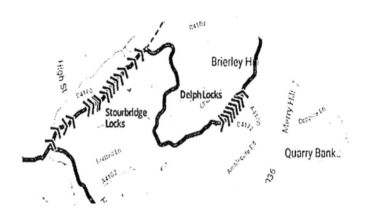

Chapter Eleven
High Bridge Too

A few hours sleep, the sunrise came
And quest began anew
To stay ahead of Walter
Was the only thing to do

So at Delph Locks, a new climb start
An interesting flight
Known as nine locks, but now, just eight
- More change to get things right

The central 'seven', (reduced to six
In 1858)
Is now a conservation site
Where tourists sit and wait

To fill the pools between the locks
See flow of waterfalls
Though now it seems, in modern day
The 'Tenth Lock' pub, it calls

Perriwillow, very tired
Felt journey was disjointed
And now the 'Tenth Lock' was denied
He felt so disappointed

But up they went, as on they must
Past stables, now restored
'till looking back, down steep hill view
Our Dwarf stepped back on board

As level out, the Round Oak site
To some is retail heaven
But factories belched out clouds of smoke
From 1857

At first, they smelted pig iron
'till the steel was introduced
And from the 1890's
Round Oak Steelworks mass produced

For nearly a full century
The toiling motioned on
'till 1982, it saw
The furnace cold, then gone

The work of Round Oak moved aside
Some sad and some were torn
A massive shopping complex grew
And Merry Hill was born

It changed the roads, the landscape too
Construction happened fast
Restaurants, bars, casino too
The Waterfront came last

Development of the canal
Received a lot of thought
Now moorings look to shops below
If different day is sought

As water flows through modern world
Marina can be found
But when you get to Round Oak Bridge
See time, again, rewound

Again, poor Perriwillow
Was denied of food and ale
They had to keep the pressure on
Ensure they would not fail

It seemed it was a long, long way
To get to the Mainline
The Wizard, on the shorter route
Could still make up some time

The Dudley No.1 Canal
Went up to Blowers Green
Then after lock, the sharpest turn
The Dwarf had ever seen

"Why can't we go through, straight ahead
It must be more direct?"
Asked Perriwillow, feeling smug
He'd read the map and checked

"We're not allowed to go through there
That's Parkhead Locks ahead
The Dudley Tunnel goes to the
Museum," Terry said

"The Black Country Museum
Is a special place to see
Reconstructed days gone by
Of life and industry

"Now, you can steer around the turn
It looks a little tight
But steer the boat as you've been shown
I'm sure you'll get it right"

So turning east at Blowers Green
Where Pumphouse, now restored
To Dudley No.2 Canal
Where fears must be ignored

Perriwillow swallowed hard
Applied what he'd been taught
He started slowly, added power
- Much better than he thought

The journey round to Windmill End
Skirts round the Netherton Hill
Where Cholera victims, buried at
St Andrews Church, lie still

Though saddened by this sombre fact
Our Dwarf remained elated
His pride in how he'd made that turn
Was vastly understated

"Well," he thought, "it's really nice
When sometimes, something works
And even on this nightmare trip
There have to be some perks"

They settled down and for a while
Were silent, nothing said
Then out in front, imposing sight
A tall, tall bridge ahead

Terry said "Now, as you go
Beneath the bridge, call out
You'll find your call will be returned
Let's go and check it out

"Officially, it's called 'High Bridge'
It stands sixty feet high
Folk know it as the 'Sounding Bridge'
And call as they pass by"

"High Bridge," said the Dwarf, in shock
"I hope this one is nice
Not like the 'High Bridge' seen before
I couldn't do that twice

"Remember bridge with telegraph pole
When Wizard did appear?
It was so very frightening
His venom, so severe"

"Oh, I remember," Terry said
Unlikely to forget
It was, indeed, a miracle
Walter hadn't caught them, yet

"Helloooooooooo," called Perriwillow
And he heard his voice rebound
"Helloooooooooo," replied the bridge
'Sarpedon's' engine echoed round

And as they passed beneath the bridge
The Crew, they felt relief
That Walter's presence hadn't showed
Their luck beyond belief

But as the stern was leaving
All the light, it left the sky
Hailstones rained upon the boat
From arch of bridge, so high

With hatred hurled upon them
As the Wizard's spell was cast
A sudden, unexpected strike
As ice cut sharp and fast

As beams of light lit up the sky
In blue and gold and green
Each twisting shape, to form the words
"Helloooooooooo, you have been seen"

Our travellers paled in horror
With the fear of spells to come
Concerned that Wally got one right
Perhaps now, not so dumb?

But still, they had no option now
And onward, they must travel
To follow liquid highway long
As journey would unravel

So past the Lodge Farm reservoir
Which led to Saltwells Wood
Where bluebells grew, each year renew
And Saltwells House once stood

Around the bends and under roads
On Dudley No.2
Through Primrose Hill and Darby End
'Sarpedon' speeding through

And so, arrive at Windmill End
Where roads and houses cease
Step back in time, where history reigns
In constant, slow release

Perriwillow stared, in awe
At all that lay around
High on the hill, Cobbs Engine House
Now stood, without a sound

Cast iron bridges, old and strong
Mark junction, now in view
Where east, at Bumble Hole
Continues Dudley No.2

The boats still run through 'Gosty Hill'
A trip you'd not forget
But none through Lappal Tunnel now
Where the Worcester and Birmingham met

"So, does mean we can't get through?"
The Dwarf asked in confusion
"Please don't say that this latest plan
Is nothing but illusion"

"Fear not," said Terry "look ahead
A newer path was made
Direct, by going underground
No need to be afraid

"The only thing we need to fear
Is where the Wizard steers
We hope to pass through chasm long
Before his crew appears

"We need to search for latest news
Of where his boat has been
To stay ahead must be our goal
We must remain unseen"

Perriwillow, unconvinced, said
"That could be quite tragic
For Wally keeps on finding us
Since he improved his magic"

"Now, don't you get disheartened,"
Terry said, "he's not that bright
Just look at all the times he's failed
He rarely gets it right

"In any case, we have no choice
There is no other way
So pray that we are still in front
For there we have to stay

"The danger lies as we emerge
We won't know much until
We make it to the other side
Appear from under hill"

Perriwillow looked confused
And knew he'd need to ask
Just what it was they had to do
For next part of their task

And so, at last, the question came
Whilst chatting on the 'gunwale'
"You've mentioned them so many times
Now tell me - what's a tunnel?"

Chapter Twelve
Tunnel & Mainline

Terry looked, in disbelief
At what the Dwarf had said
"You've never heard of tunnels?"
Perriwillow shook his head

They take a shortcut, underground
A path cut through the stone
This one, from 1858
A feat of flesh and bone

The last of major tunnels built
It's high and long and wide
Had gas lights when it first was built
And towpaths, either side

It eased the traffic going through
From Dudley No.1
Put Netherton upon the map
By hiding from the sun

The chasm drawing closer, as
The Dwarf he shook with fear
When darkness enveloped the boat
- No gas lights shone in here

"Now don't be silly," Terry said
"For go through here we must
These days, we use a tunnel light
Your eyes, they will adjust

"And if you stare just straight ahead
As straight this tunnel be
You'll see the end, just waiting there
To set 'Sarpedon' free"

Perriwillow breathed anew
He didn't feel so scared
He simply hadn't understood
And hadn't been prepared

The tunnel, nearly two miles long
Gave time to look around
At ghostly shadows, lurking deep
And engines echoed sound

The murky glow of headlight
And the smell of dampened air
The Dwarf had never dreamed
That this existed anywhere

If ever he could make it home
Oh, what a tale to tell
But getting home was proving tough
- On this, he should not dwell

So onward, forward, yard by yard
They moved toward the light
'till most of darkness lay behind
And end was clear in sight

'Sarpedon' shot from twilight
She emerged to light of day
Though very different scenery
A dark, industrial way

The Netherton Tunnel Branch Canal
Continues, very short
Under Old Mainline aqueduct
Then on, to Dudley Port

"This junction is the one to watch,"
Said Terry, "who can guess
Where Wally is – in front, behind
This could end in a mess

"He might be right there waiting
And cut off the path we seek
Let's hope that time is on our side
And Wizard's power is weak"

They soon approached an iron bridge
Which marked where waters meet
There was, indeed, a boat ahead
Where arm was raised to greet

Now, was this Friend, or was it Foe?
In gesture quite confusing
For after wrecking hire boat
What craft was Walter using?

Terry seemed to be relaxed
When saw who was there waiting
He raised a hand in friendly wave
No sign of hesitating

"Look," he said, "it's 'Tardebigge'
My friend is on the stern
I'm hoping that he has some news
And Wizard's route we'll learn"

"Go quickly," said the steerer
"You'll find Walter close behind
You'd better get a move on
As he's feeling quite unkind"

"What vessel is he using now?
It's something we should know,"
Said Terry, "Though I dread to think
I hope it's something slow"

"Well, after Wally's escapade
Upon the '21'
There's few will lend, or hire a craft
He could rely upon

"It seems he's paid a fortune
Just to borrow tiny boat
The owner's not expecting it
To come back home afloat

"It's powered by an outboard
And the Wizard thinks it's mighty
But overloaded with his Crew
The steering's somewhat flighty"

"I guess we'd better get ahead,"
Said Terry, "let's make haste
A little boat can move quite fast
We have no time to waste"

Bernard, steering 'Tardebigge'
Could not supress a smile
"Quite fast between the accidents
They may still be a while

"It seems they've bounced from bank to bank
Their steering hardly stable
Then gaining speed when holding straight
As fast as boat were able"

It was a most amusing thought
To think of Wizard's Crew
Now weaving down the long canal
Still having not a clue

"But that won't get us anywhere,"
Said Terry, "let's get going
We need to work out what to do
To keep our journey flowing"

They set out east, to Gas Street
Now the plan was taking shape
They had to know the Wizard's route
To make a clean escape

Bernard went the other way
To meet with Walter's path
To try and cause distraction and
Report the aftermath

'Sarpedon' got to Gas Street
Just as fast as she could move
Their plan, it needed tactics
For their chances to improve

Terry moored at Oozells Street
Well hidden in The Loop
Then out on foot, they waited
For the Wizard's circus troupe

It wasn't long 'till they arrived
Heard well before were seen
The shouting and the arguing
Was not a good routine

"So, which way do you think they'll go?"
Said Perriwillow next
"I hope that they don't notice us
Old Wally must be vexed"

"We'll hide around this corner, here,"
Said Terry, with a grin
"That way, we'll see their antics
In a way that saves our skin"

The Wizard and his crew appeared
Packed onto 'Annie Rose'
And in the rush of choosing route
It seems they'd come to blows

So at the junction 'roundabout'
The scene was heaven sent
They couldn't choose, they couldn't steer
- So round and round they went

The narrowboat was twenty feet
And handled light as feather
So left, ahead, then where they'd been
Would they go round forever?

At last, poor Walter raised his wand
As route he hoped to pick
His ashen face was tinged with green
He felt he might be sick

"Stop!" he yelled, the boat did pause
Ceased spinning round and round
Then 'Annie Rose' shot through a bridge
On Fazeley route now bound

"It seems they're going that way,"
Said the Dwarf, "the lock gate's open
So let's get moving straight away
Before more spells get spoken"

"I hope he doesn't use more spells
In aim to boost his power,"
Said Terry, "Wally's headed off
Beneath the BT Tower"

'Sarpedon', waiting patiently
They soon were on their way
And straight ahead, past boats and bars
No time to waste the day

In leaving of the BCN
The City left behind
On Worcester and Birmingham Canal
What dangers would they find?

So round the sharp right-angled bend
To Edgbaston they veer
And through a tiny tunnel, where
Perriwillow had a steer

For mile on mile, head southward
With the railway keeping pace
It followed path, along canal
Though these days, win each race

Where industry would once have stood
Now learning is the key
Where students walk and set the scene
At university

Just south of here, at Selly Oak
Is site of intersection
Where Dudley Branch had once emerged
Now viewed with much affection

Though as we know that road was hard
So much that did go wrong
Where Lappal Tunnel once emerged
With tiny bore, so long

"It would have been a shorter route,"
Said Terry, "but I doubt
That you'd have liked that tunnel long
You'd fear of getting out!"

So, on they went, another mile
And then the Dwarf cried out
"A purple railway station, tell me
What's that all about?"

"That is the site of Cadbury Works
And chocolate there is made
Bournville is where employees lived
As part of getting paid"

Perriwillow's eyes lit up
At thought of chocolate, sweet
"Fear not, my friend, it's not too long
Before we stop and eat"

"I'm very pleased," the Dwarf replied
"Though day's not been that long
It seems forever since we stopped
And food would keep me strong"

It wasn't long before they reached
Kings Norton Junction, where
On turning east, through guillotine lock
They soon could eat their share

Along the Stratford-on Avon Canal
Just four miles left to glide
They pass through Brandwood Tunnel
Not too long 'till be inside

So dreaming of an alehouse
Weary travellers forged ahead
'till stopped at 'Shirley Drawbridge' pub
In search of food, then bed

They ate their fill and drank some ale
With not a lot to say
Then lay their heads in dreamless sleep
To face tomorrows day

Chapter Thirteen
Going Down

Our weary travellers, rested now
Awoke when day was new
With heartened souls they forged ahead
Now knowing what to do

They knew where they were heading
And, no time for them to lose
It seemed they had the quickest route
Through luck they didn't choose

The Wizard still had choice and if
He went the quickest way
To where paths meet, he'd stay behind
By roughly half a day

There was another option, where
He'd sneak up, unannounced
Come from behind, or Crew ahead
In ambush, where they pounced

This, Terry found unlikely
For it was the longest route
And Wally's Crew were not the best
At steering hot pursuit

"It's going to be a long few days,"
Said Terry, "let's get working
There's lots of locks and sometimes shocks
There'll be no time for shirking"

Perriwillow didn't care
At last, they were ahead
It seemed there was a tiny chance
He wouldn't go home dead

They passed through Shirley Drawbridge
Where you need a special key
Perriwillow turned the lock
"There's just no stopping me!"

Terry thought how nice it was
To see Dwarf's spirits rise
He always looked so miserable
This was a nice surprise

The risks were high, the dangers worse
But now, there was some hope
Perhaps they'd meet some luck
Before they found a slippery slope?

A few more miles of countryside
Then lock on lock they met
And so, did start a downward hill
Our Dwarf would ne'er forget

The Lapworth flight was soon begun
With bridges halved and split
Allowing tow rope to pass through
So horse not slowed a bit

Much opening and close of gates
A massive undertaking
To Kingswood Junction, locks go down
'till windlass arm was aching

Canal goes on to Stratford
But our travellers change the pace
Turn onto the Grand Union
Such a very different place

As out of narrow lock they passed
The waterway, it changed
From small and quaint, without restraint
The backdrop was exchanged

"It's massive," Perriwillow said
"Why has it gone so wide?"
"My little friend, you've lots to learn"
- Poor Perriwillow sighed

"I guess that means there's lots of things
To scare me half to death?
You'll tell me not to be so scared
- I wouldn't hold your breath"

On turning right, they breathed relief
Glad Walter wasn't there
'twas far more likely that he'd crashed
But still, no time to spare

The next six miles, in silence passed
The Dwarf, full of elation
Through Shrewley Tunnel, wooded hills
And past Hatton Rail Station

Terry spoke with serious tone
"Prepare yourself for shock
You won't have seen the like before
On sight of your next lock"

"I've seen a lot of locks before
So what could be so bad?"
The Dwarf retorted sharply
"After all the frights I've had"

"It's not that it is bad at all
But might not seem inviting
It might not be what you expect
- You might find it exciting

"I hope you're full of energy
To tackle yonder flight
Let's say it's somewhat larger
In its length and width and height"

Poor Perriwillow disbelieved
But ended up agreeing
When stand at top of Hatton Flight
- What was it he was seeing?

The locks they were, well, twice as wide
Two boats went in together
Two massive gates at either end
Dwarf didn't feel too clever

"How will I push those gates so big
They're just as tall as me?"
Said Perriwillow, feeling glum
And tiny as could be

"You know you're strong," said Terry
"And you're muscles are not weak
You operate locks just the same
It's mostly good technique"

Terry had to teach the Dwarf
How strange, round paddles wound
With many, many, many turns
To rise without a sound

Then when time came to close them down
The jewel in the crown
Release the catch and watch
- The paddle quietly goes down

The locks, they number twenty-one
Spread over just two miles
They rise 146 feet
A mix of frowns and smiles

Flight opened in 1934
A thousand men to build
New concrete locks replaced the old
Held two boats as they filled

'Stairway to heaven' is how it's known
- At start, won't feel so good
But feel accomplished, once you're done
As well deserved, you should

And so, 'Sarpedon' made descent
They worked without delay
A busy flight, as leave each lock
Folk come the other way

"That's handy," Terry told the Dwarf
"No need to shut the gates
As up they come, they do the same
So open lock awaits

"It saves us lots of energy
And also saves us time
It really makes the difference
Between feeling tired or fine"

Because they were in double locks
They shared the lock and graft
Thus aided by another Crew
A second heritage craft

'Gerald', built by Stewart and Lloyd
Fleet number '108'
Well steered by Barry, led the way
Through every pound and gate

Barry's wife, she did the locks
No problem there at all
Showed Perriwillow all the tricks
- No need of being tall

They reached the bottom lock at last
Though quicker than expected
"That was a nice surprise," said Dwarf
As fears he recollected

Jenny, Barry's wife, replied
"'twas good today, although
Sometimes you pair with novice folk
Who make it very slow"

"I know just what you mean,"
Said Perriwillow, thinking quick
"There's some who seem to steer a boat
Just like a lunatic"

Of course, he'd thought of Wally
Wondered where the Fiend had gone?
"Just keep on going, Dwarf, me lad"
He thought, don't dwell upon

And so, proceed past Saltisford Arm
Where sharp left turn is done
- But don't go straight ahead
Resulting chaos isn't fun

Here lies the town of Warwick, where
Some like to look around
It is a place both old and new
Surviving castle found

'Gerald' led, intending stop
With hope that moorings there
In luck, no-one had tied up first
Moored up with room to spare

The day, it had been very long
And Perriwillow faltered
His muscles hurt, his head it ached
His mood had now been altered

His spirits started on a high
But now, he felt dismayed
The only thing that cheered him up
Were friendships, new, he'd made

Barry came and shook his hand
"Well done, my little fellow
Time to relax, to eat and drink
An evening that is mellow

"Tomorrow is another day
Tonight, relax, enjoy
Good ale and food, good company
Where no-one will annoy"

The 'Cape of Good Hope' welcomed them
With feeling of goodwill
And Perriwillow, full of cheer
Did eat and drink his fill

"Goodnight Barry, Jenny too
Much thanks for company
I'm sure tomorrow's bound to bring
A glorious day to see"

So Terry guided Dwarf to boat
To sleep off evenings joy
And gather strength, for tactics new
Where brains they must employ

Chapter Fourteen
Up The Hill To Braunston

When they awoke, the rain it fell
As nasty, soaking drizzle
But Perriwillow soon cheered up
When breakfast pan did sizzle

He was a little groggy still
From tankards full of ale
But felt restored and ready
To continue homeward trail

Breakfast, very welcome
To the Dwarf, was not denied
Devouring plate of sausage, eggs
And bread that had been fried

Terry watched a happy
Perriwillow tucking in
It seemed a million years ago
Since Dwarf kept falling in

Reflecting on the early days
When seeds of tale first sown
From frightened Boy to Dwarfling man
In many ways had grown

Perriwillow raised his head
A wise look in his eyes
He saw a sadness Terry
Couldn't manage to disguise

"You too imagine journeys end
And different things to fear
That time we've planned, when I go home
And you will still be here

"When this adventure we began
And I was quite naive
I couldn't face existence trapped
Where I could never leave

"But over time, I've learnt that fate
Which sometimes seems unkind
Can leave a new perspective
Which you're sad to leave behind

"So let's enjoy what life can bring
This isn't over, yet
I may not even make it home
If Walter's wish be met"

They laughed awhile and past reflection
Now replaced by mirth
As 'Gerald's' engine sprang to life
To bring them back to earth

"Come on," said Barry, "time to go
You know we must make haste
We know the Wizard's slow and daft
But still, no time to waste"

They started down through both Cape Locks
Then Leamington on the way
From near and far, Victorian spa
Sought after in its day

Through wooded cutting, Radford hides
And urban sights are gone
Then climb again at Radford Lock
Uphill and on and on

Fosse Locks, Wood Lock, Longhole Bridge
In bid to win the race
Through Welsh Road Lock, then Bascote
Where Dwarf meets his first staircase

Perriwillow, fascinated
Always something strange
It seemed each time he knew the drill
The rules would somehow change

Barry said, "The staircase lock
Needs thought if you are wise
Ascending, make sure locks above
Are full, or risk surprise

"If lock above is empty
There's no water left to flow
Down into where your boat awaits
To rise, then out you go"

So in they went, the pair of boats
Together, side by side
Look up, the chamber full, but Barry
Took it in his stride

The Dwarf, he wasn't quite so sure
He felt this nagging fear
That all the water would cascade
And sink the boats down here

Of course, that didn't happen here
And safely, up they went
Emerging soon, now at the top
Completing the ascent

"That's four more locks out of the way,"
Said Terry, "now we're steaming
We'll be in Braunston by tonight
Unless we start daydreaming"

So, on they went, to Cuttle
Through Long Itchington they moved
Where pub on pub they passed
- Poor Perriwillow disapproved

"Now don't go getting lazy
It's too early in the day
You haven't earned your food or ale
So let's get underway

"We're at the base of Stockton Locks,"
Said Terry, "let's not falter
Although we should be well ahead
Don't want to meet with Walter"

The double locks, they climbed ahead
Old narrow locks beside
More evidence of progress new
Historic, changing tide

The quarries dug Blue Lias clay
Jurassic fossils found
Cement made here was used to make
The Thames Embankment sound

So through Blue Lias Road Bridge
Where in recent years, things changed
And folk who once bought narrowboats
For widebeam boats exchanged

The bridge is only twelve feet wide
So if misread the map
Be unaware that boat too wide
- Too late, caught in the trap

There's some who have got wedged in there
Gongoozlers come for miles
To stand and gawp, take photographs
Misfortune causing smiles

Although, it isn't funny
If a queue of folk, delayed
From both directions, get too keen
To show they are dismayed

But our brave Crew, on narrowboats
Went through with room to spare
And on they went, to top of flight
No drama anywhere

An empty landscape carries on
With nothing much to see
A big marina, Calcutt Locks
Not many, only three

It wasn't long to Napton
Where Oxford Canal is met
The Wizard, not expected
For, he shouldn't be here yet

But just in case, it seemed the best
That 'Gerald' edged out first
To check the junction, look each way
'twas right to fear the worst

No sign of Wizard, or his Crew
And safely turning east
Through Lower Shuckburgh, Wolfhampcote
- Not long 'till pub and feast

"I think we'll stop at Puddle Banks,"
Said Terry, "let's take care
If we emerge at Braunston Turn
The Wizard may be there

"And if he is not far away
Come past while we are sleeping
We don't want to be killed in bed
When watch we are not keeping"

"I don't agree," the Dwarf cried out
"If Wally gets ahead
We'll lose advantage that we've gained
Let's try and hide instead"

"You're getting wise, my little friend,"
Said Terry, "Let's pass through
The Braunston Turn, where all roads meet
It seems the thing to do"

But as they moved toward The Turn
Where 'Gerald' led the way
They heard a voice from towpath side
"I've somewhere you can stay

"The Wizard won't be here today
It seems he was detained
He caused some bother with a spell
And had to be restrained

"He got a bit unruly
As his innocence protested
Upsetting of an officer
Saw Wally get arrested"

At thought of Walter, in a cell
When story Man did mention
Our travellers couldn't stifle mirth
It really eased the tension

The man directed them ahead
They did as they were bidden
"Moor on the bank, behind 'The Rat'
Your boats will be well hidden

"My name is Pete, so pleased to meet
With you, I've heard your tale
I'd like to welcome you to 'Rat'
And offer food and ale"

Our tired friends were very pleased
That safety they had found
A friendly face, a hearty meal
And comfort, all around

Another evening of good cheer
Perriwillow felt well blessed
He raised his glass at every toast
And laughed when some did jest

Though in a corner of his mind
The strangest thoughts did grow
He didn't understand it
But it made him feel aglow

For as they'd steered around the turn
With wonder, he did see
A shimmering halo, under bridge
Whatever could it be?

Maybe, he had imagined it?
Maybe, he was just tired?
Maybe, he was just dreaming
Or his brain was over-wired?

'twas best that he forget, but still
The images persist
Within his minds reflection
- See 'Dwarf City', through the mist

Chapter Fifteen
What Walter Did Next

The last time we saw Walter
He was feeling rather green
As 'Annie Rose' chose Fazeley path
Though Walter wasn't keen

He had intended other route
Which nasty Dwarf had taken
"But this boat is un-steerable"
- Directions he'd mistaken

The topmost lock at Farmers Bridge
Was open, gates ajar
The boat shot in at rocket speed
Crowds scattered near and far

By miracle, he missed the sides
Shot clean into the lock
Forgot reverse, no chance to slow
As bottom gate took shock

The Mottley Crew performed as one
Gates shut and paddles wound
As floodgates opened, Wizard screamed
In fear that he'd be drowned

He really couldn't steer the boat
His street cred faded fast
From side to side he weaved
Convinced this day would be his last

He had prepared to scold the crew
For going down the flight
But seemed he was committed
Best pretend he'd got it right

"This is the better way," he cried
"I'm glad we chose this path"
The Mottley Crew, not so convinced
Filled Walter full of wrath

They bumped and weaved, 'till underneath
Refurbished multi-storey
Once part of 'BT' offices
Which in their day, held glory

A holding pool, beside the lock
Brought dreams of pool to swim
But pure surprise, though day so hot
One Mottley Crew jumped in

"It's not a pool where you can swim,"
Cried Walter, with a yell
"Get out of there!" too late
Remaining Crew jumped in as well

The Wizard was incensed with rage
His Crew had run amok
What's more, who'd work the paddles now
Release him from the lock?

Much whooping, shouting, cries of mirth
From Crew annoyed him more
"They'll do just what I say," he sneered
"I'll settle soon this score"

Walter raised the fated wand
It stopped the antics dead
The Mottley Crew, they scattered wide
As air hung still, in dread

The water boiled, a mighty crack
Then debris raining down
The Grinning Fiend on 'Annie Rose'
Had really gone to town

He didn't seem remorseful
At the mess that had been made
Be sure that he had never thought
Of price that would be paid

The Mottley Crew had disappeared
Anticipating trouble
If Walter didn't kill them first
Someone would burst his bubble

And sure enough, it happened
In an armed Police attack
"Get off the boat, lie on the floor
With hands behind your back!"

Walter wasn't having it
"There's nothing wrong," he said
"Don't mess with me" and then he saw
Guns pointed at his head

"I said get down upon the floor,"
Again the sternest voice
"There's no discussion, no request
I'm giving you no choice"

Wally did as he was bid
Request could not deny
Substandard magic couldn't help
He didn't want to die

The Officer, he spoke again
In voice that didn't falter
He puffed his chest, an even
Bigger 'Jobsworth' than our Walter

"You can't go round just casting spells
As down the 'cut' you go
We don't allow no terrorists
- It's Birmingham you know"

The Mottley Crew, now hovering
This scene was cast in gold
A rare event, with Wally doing
What he had been told

The crew were in hysterics now
They laughed so hard, they cried
Seems even 'Annie Rose' joined in
She rocked from side to side

"I'm going to arrest you, Mate,"
The 'Jobsworth' carried on
"Impounding of your vessel, too
As law we act upon

"Who knows what you are carrying?
What dangers do you haul?"
"Not much," thought Walter, little
Could be stashed in boat so small

"We've seen it all before," said 'Jobsworth'
Filled with true elation
"Now, cuff him Lads, impound the boat
And take him down the station"

The Wizard, he was led away
Excuses were rebuffed
The Mottley Crew looked on at Walter
Captured, held and cuffed

'Annie Rose', she handled well
With new, experienced steerer
The fact that Wally couldn't 'drive'
Could not have been made clearer

So Walter down the station went
And 'Annie Rose' impounded
'till explanations had been made
The Wizard's Mob were grounded

Let's not go into detail and
Let's keep the tale quite sparse
Let's just assume that Wally talked
His way out of the farce

The charge for wasting 'Coppers' time
Held warnings stern and tragic
Though seemed that Wally's only crime
Was practicing bad magic

Poor 'Annie Rose' was torn apart
To look for goods unlawful
And now, the price to pay reveal
For damage that was awful

Remember, boat was only hired
For quite exorbitant fee?
So now, returned to owner
- Meet the savvy Captain 'P'

The man collected 'Annie Rose'
Released her from the station
They wouldn't let the Wizard go
'till he'd paid compensation

Captain 'P', his eyes lit up
Was what he heard for real?
"We're going to need another boat
Can you do another deal?"

"My Son's boat is available
But damage was extensive
To 'Annie Rose', so let's be clear
This deal will be expensive"

Walter, out of options now
In cash was quickly paying
In haste to go, pursue the Dwarf
He wanted no delaying

Captain 'P' was happy
As financial loss had faded
The bonus here, his prospects
For retirement had upgraded

So very soon, they journeyed on
The Wizard and his Mob
On 'Mr Badger', a bigger craft
More suited to the job

At least, in her stability
Propulsion and her space
But her 'look' was rather obvious
She lacked a certain grace

"I wanted anonymity,"
Said Walter, "tell me how
I sneak around, unseen, with that
Great figurehead on the bow?"

Indeed, the model, rather large
With origin unclear
Would herald presence, far and wide
When best to disappear

The boat belonged to 'Crystal Karl'
The son of Captain 'P'
Said Karl, "Don't change or break my boat
Or you'll answer to me"

The Wizard deemed to just ignore
The things he couldn't alter
And after all, the figurehead
It looked a lot like Walter

The next few days were hectic
And as all, no doubt, expected
The journey, long, would leave a trail
Where many were affected

Wally steered from time to time
Engrossed in his endeavour
Through Aston, down to Salford went
His skill as bad as ever

Through Erdington and Tyburn
Then to Minworth, Curdworth too
With lots of locks and many miles
Of bashing, crashing through

The route choice made at Fazeley
Was without a major fight
'twas pointed out from passing boat
So Walter got it right

A messy turn toward Glascote
'Mr Badger', underway
Rose to the top lock, trouble free
This made the Wizard's day

"I think I've found the boat for me,"
Said Walter, "no more trouble"
The Mottley Crew looked on in mirth
Another broken bubble?

Through Tamworth, down to Alvecote
Large Marina, with a pub
The 'Samuel Barlow' nestled there
A working, social hub

The 'Greyhound', 'Captain Cargo'
Steered by Malcolm, was observed
The Wizard was oblivious
His ego well preserved

The workboat crews were 'family'
But Walter didn't know
That news of 'Mr Badger'
Soon to Dwarf and Man would go

So on went 'Mr Badger', as
Through day and night they go
Just like the 'Fly Boats' used to do
No time to stop, or slow

Past Pooley Hall and Polesworth
Then to Atherstone flight of locks
Where Crew, in trepidation feared
For damage, loss and shocks

The news of Wally's steering style
Had prompted urgent need
So volunteers who worked the locks
Came running at full speed

"And so they should," said Walter
"Well, I am a VIP,"
He puffed his chest and waved his arm
"Most folk have heard of me"

The volunteers who saw the arm
Go up, as if in magic
Had seen the news of Birmingham
And dreaded spell so tragic

They wound the paddles, opened gates
In haste, they didn't stop
Disaster didn't happen
- 'Mr Badger' reached the top

In record time, they cleared the flight
And off toward Mancetter
Then Hartshill and Nuneaton town
Things couldn't go much better

The Ashby flows from Marston turn
Its industry outdated
But Walter went toward 'Charity Dock'
Where many boats have waited

"Oi, Mate, do you want to flog your boat?"
A voice from Dock cried out
"I think you'd fit quite well in here
Do you want to sort it out?"

Walter, so insulted, said
"My craft is good and sound"
Revved 'Mr Badger's' 'BMC'
And black smoke swirled around

From there, he was more careful
As the smoke made him concerned
Past Bedworth, through to Hawkesbury
Where at Sutton Stop, they turned

The horseshoe turn, eventful and
In truth, it isn't child's play
But Walter, revved with gung-ho power
Was bound to take the hard way

He started off quite slowly
So the bow was turning well
'till Wally tried a show-off trick
That caused his Crew to yell

"Back off," said one, another hid
Beneath the cabin top
A crowd appeared from Greyhound pub
As Walter tried to stop

But 'Mr Badger' hurtled on
Like fastest craft afloat
The figurehead, upon the bow
Now T-boned shiny boat

Walter, as we've come to know
Soon rose above his station
But outcome, as expected
Soon involved more compensation

The Wizard, now, had seen enough
And claimed of being tired
He went to bed, told Mottley Crew
To motor, as required

Now down the dark Oxford Canal
And on to Stretton Stop
Where swing bridge by the 'Rose Boats' fleet
Was pushed and shoved a lot

Past Brinklow Arm, where old boats went
To mostly be renewed
Then Newbold, where in years now past
Fluorescent lights were viewed

So on through Rugby, Clifton Wharf
And through Hillmorton flight
Where climbing rise in sets of two
So peaceful there at night

A moonlight trip to Braunston
As the Wizard soundly slept
Now dreaming that, at break of day
Our Dwarf he'd intercept

Chapter Sixteen
The Magic of Braunston

Perriwillow rose at dawn
Head filled with plans anew
His secret smile held promise
Of the things he hoped to do

He'd lain awake most of the night
In thinking what he'd seen
'Dwarf City', hiding in the mist
As worlds he stood between

The others slept, he took a walk
Completely undecided
At what he'd do if Braunston Turn
Was where the worlds divided

They'd planned to find the Witch from Wales
To help him on his way
But if the path were now revealed
He'd have to leave today

To go without his fond farewells
Would leave him sad and broken
But yes, he'd have to go right now
If shimmering path lay open

His friends might think he'd run away
Without a last goodbye
The thought that he'd desert the team
Made Perriwillow cry

But still, he had to face the fact
That home he might return
"So best foot forward, Dwarf me Lad
If truth you're going to learn"

The Dwarf walked slowly to The Turn
To check for shimmering mist
To see if he'd imagined that
The worlds could co-exist

He stared at where the way had formed
Part willing, part in dread
To see if doorway was for real
Or made up in his head?

The air it stirred; a haze appeared
And swirling mist unfurled
Reality appeared to bend
Revealed the other world

"'Dwarf City'," Perriwillow whispered
Totally in awe
But voice behind, "I've got you now
You'll run from me no more"

Perriwillow froze in fear
Close to the Wizard's hand
The only way was forward
Through the door to other land

The Dwarf stepped forward bravely
Said, "Goodbye, my friends, farewell
I wish that you were here to see
Escape, from Wizard's spell"

At second step, he reached the gate
Prepared to step straight through
But Walter pulled him backwards
- What a rotten thing to do

"I've told you once, I've got you!"
"No you haven't!" Dwarf replied
He elbowed Walter in the ribs
Ran for the other side

The Dwarf, now free of Walter
(Who now fell into the 'cut')
Dived clean toward the other world
- Too late, the gate slammed shut

The Dwarf regained composure
Which just kept him on his feet
But now, with nowhere left to run
No road to where paths meet

The Mottley Crew came running in
To aid the Wizard's plight
(Pulled Walter out of wet canal
'twas quite a funny sight)

Perriwillow waited
Now quite certain he would die
In bridge hole, at the junction
There was nothing left to try

What happened next amazed him
As a 'Pusher Tug' came through
On 'Constance', he was scooped aboard
By Terry and the crew

They motored fast and flighty
'till quite clear of Wizard's Clan
'Sarpedon', she was moving now
Awaiting Dwarf and Man

'Constance Tug' was motoring
As fast as she could go
Pete, now steering faster
- Terry hoped that he would slow

For Dwarf was thrown from 'Constance'
With no grace or style for now
Poor Perriwillow landed hard
Upon 'Sarpedon's' bow

The Dwarf now safe and 'Constance' slowed
As Pete made manic turn
He pulled aside 'Sarpedon'
Terry stepped upon her stern

Barry held 'Sarpedon' straight
As Pete, he waved farewell
And headed off, to make some waves
Diverting Wizard's spell

Perriwillow caught his breath
His street cred would revive
For now, he just felt grateful
He'd got out of this alive

Back on the stern, our Dwarf appeared
Unscathed from all the fright
Though shaken from the magic stuff
That happened overnight

He checked on what was happening
Now safely back on board
Discussed a plan to get ahead
Where next to be explored

The friends discussed the new events
Compared what each one saw
How Perriwillow's home appeared
But sadly, now, no more

They had to find the Goodly Witch
To help them on their way
It seemed for now, 'Dwarf City's' gates
Were closed and gone, today

Perriwillow, deep in thought
Felt need to speak at last
"Why can't we use the 'Constance Tug'?
She'd get there very fast"

Awhile in thought, then Terry spoke
"My friend, it's more than speed
The 'Pusher Tug' cannot provide
The other things you need

"Nowhere to sleep, nowhere to go
To keep out of the weather
Her job is pushing boats along
By strapping them together"

Dwarf wound 'Sarpedon's' engine up
Escape from new disaster
The heavy boat increased her speed
Propeller turning faster

It wasn't long before a shout
From man, with fist and frown
"It's not a blooming race, you know
Why don't you slow her down?"

"There you go," said Terry,
"See, so if too fast you steer
You won't sneak past unnoticed
And your plans become quite clear

"You'll be as bad as Walter
Be a nuisance and a pest
No skill, no morals, nothing like
A boatman at his best"

Perriwillow thought, in part
He'd rather save his skin
But in the end, he saw the sense
And pride of fitting in

"Sorry mate," the Dwarf called out
"The Wizard's close behind
Forgot to be considerate
Too much was on my mind"

The man acknowledged, raised his hand
"Apology accepted"
How things had changed in recent years
He sadly recollected

'Sarpedon' slowed down nicely now
But Terry hit reverse
A 'widebeam cruiser' blocked the way
Today was getting worse

"Hold tighter," Terry shouted,
"As there's no more you can do!"
By no less than a miracle
'Kanthaka' shot straight through

"Sorry Mate, I didn't see
Your boat, but all is fine
Just call me Aemonn, stop and have
A drink with me next time"

The Man and Dwarf were speechless
Though somewhat of a relief
'Kanthaka' weaved up wide canal
They watched, in disbelief

For Aemonn stopped the Mottley Crew
'Kanthaka' blocked their way
So 'Mr Badger' couldn't catch
'Sarpedon' underway

Past Braunston Marina, Dwarf goes on
Boats quiet, feigning sleep
"Until the old boats come along
It's chaos for a week

"Each year in June," smiled Barry
"Lots of Boat Folk have some fun
At Braunston Historic Rally
Your 'Sarpedon', she should come

"There are parades for all to see
With brass and paint so bright
'Gerald' always joins them
And we party every night"

"That sounds a million miles away
Without this fear and strife,"
Said Perriwillow, "How I'd like
A day within that life"

"No time for dreaming," Terry said
"We've got too far to go
I know it seems impossible
But hold the tale of woe"

So onward now, past Redshaw's Yard
Where folk worked day and night
To keep old engines running
Just beneath the Braunston flight

Jenny, at the bottom lock
Had set one gate ajar
So on and up the flight of six
It wasn't very far

"Where is 'Gerald'?" cried the Dwarf
"You can't leave her behind"
"She's moored with 'Rat'," said Jenny
"Pete, he said he didn't mind

"We're through with mad adventure
As although we've done our best
We're not as young as we once were
We really need a rest"

Perriwillow was upset
As friends he had to leave
But understood that all could use
A peaceful, calm reprieve

"We found the gate," said Terry
"And the Witch may hold the key
You never know, we might be back
You'll have to wait and see"

"Now, best be gone," said Barry
"As you've gained a decent lead
But Walter's on the move again
So onward, at full speed"

"But with consideration"
Perriwillow shared a grin
As Terry said, "There's times when I
Preferred you falling in"

It seemed a long, long time ago
When journey first began
When accidental friendship grew
Between the Dwarf and Man

It wasn't very long before
The wooded cut closed in
With dampened air and shadowed light
The chill, it did begin

"We'd better put some lights on"
Terry said, stood on the gunwale
As Perriwillow shook his head
"Another blinking tunnel!"

Chapter Seventeen
Toward The Goodly Witch

At this stage, our roaming Dwarf
Was happy underground
An expert hand in tunnel deep
To Goodly Witch now bound

A tighter space, a different feel
So dark and dank and cold
Opened in 1796
This tunnel, very old

Construction slowed, mistakes were made
Which leaves a slight 'S' bend
2042 yards inside
And hard to see the end

No towpath for a horse to walk
A track goes over hill
Past brick-built shafts which vent the air
From tunnel, venting still

"Braunston is important
In the boatmen's history,"
Said Terry, "records in the church
Reveal much mystery

"Like marriages and births and deaths
Within 'All Saints' church door
And nine sad deaths from cholera
In 1834"

'Sarpedon', free of moored up boats
Could now increase her speed
For after swim in tunnel long
Advantage they would need

The narrow tunnel, on and on
No ghostly sights did see
The chasm clear, so motor on
And from the Wizard flee

It all was going very well
No sight of Mob at stern
And every boat length, every yard
Pushed forward, truth to learn

The darkness enveloped their thoughts
So full of hope and fear
With mixed emotions, scarring deep
From things which brought Dwarf here

There must have been a reason
Fate inflicted him with magic
But Perriwillow wished it didn't
Have to be so tragic

For magic was of fairy dust
Where wishes could come true
But no, he got the darker kind
Which killed him and his Crew

He snapped himself out of those thoughts
For still, they were in front
And true, he felt excitement
When the Wizard pulled a stunt

No lighted boats approached them
Which could slow them on their way
So getting to the Goodly Witch
Might still be done today

But nothing goes that smoothly here
And soon, the way so clear
Was blocked by boat, which crawled along
- Why go so slow in here?

The steerer moved erratically
And veered from side to side
With no control, from wall to wall
The poor boat did collide

Perriwillow throttled back
He tutted, with a frown
He hadn't planned to get held up
Or have to slow right down

"What is that idiot doing here?
He's holding up the flow
Can't steer the boat – he's hopeless
And we need to pass and go"

"Everybody has to learn
Think back, not very long,"
Said Terry, "when you couldn't steer
And everything went wrong"

First he smiled and then, he laughed
His voice full of elation
"It seems that now, at last you know
The source of my frustration"

The Dwarf went very quiet
It had made him feel quite glad
That Terry taught him well, "But still
I wasn't quite that bad?"

"That's down to an opinion,"
Laughing man supressed a grin
"You had a different habit though
You kept on falling in"

And so, they had to follow
Though the boat was barely moving
By now, the steerer, terrified
Showed no signs of improving

Bang and bump, from side to side
No chance of getting past
So patience was a virtue
'till the end in sight, at last

But at the stern, a noise behind
Much shouting, engine loud
Seems luck was running out, it was
The Wizard's Mottley Crowd

They weren't that close, not yet at least
But gaining, ever faster
"Let's hope he doesn't cast a spell,"
Said Terry, "pure disaster"

The boat in front was nearly out
Almost in daylight air
'Sarpedon' snuggled close behind
The tension hard to bear

Then in a heartbeat, way was clear
The Dwarf could overtake
Shot out of tunnel, revved her hard
And left them in her wake

"Why did you have to be like that?"
Said Steerer, "You're so rude
I'm here on holiday, you know
No need for attitude"

Perriwillow didn't slow
The reprimand unheard
'Sarpedon's' engine, far too loud
To hear a single word

Back in the light, no boat ahead
One thing they all agreed
With 'Mr Badger' close behind
They must increase their lead

They looked behind and saw the Mob
Emerge from underground
And moving in for overtake
So Dwarf could soon be found

But fate, it often lends a hand
Poor Man on Holiday
Saw Wizard and his Scary Crew
- And tried to run away

In fearing for his life and
Being scared, no, terrified
He left the tiller, boat in gear
And locked himself inside

Not the wisest move to make
For boat without a steerer
Veered off its course, in Walter's path
As overtake got nearer

The havoc, worse than average
Though seen only from a distance
As now, 'Sarpedon's' crew sped up
At Terry's strong insistence

"We've got to get through Buckby Locks
And distance we must gain
Though seems that they'll be quite a while
In trouble they remain"

So motor on and looking back
At carnage unsurprising
"Maybe they've blown her up" said Dwarf
On seeing smoke, now rising

There wasn't time to worry much
Or watch the Wizard's spite
No doubt he would apportion blame
- But onward, to the flight

The wooded cut had opened out
Now parting of the way
At Norton Junction, Leicester Line
- But don't go there today

Down Buckby Flight, they battled through
Past pumphouse and a pub
No promise now of popping in
To join the social hub

Perriwillow ran ahead
Worked hard until the end
He wished that Jenny had come too
He missed his 'locking friend'

So close to roads and railway lines
Like snapshots held in time
The Dwarf thought "What of other worlds
And journeys such as mine"

But travel on, through bottom lock
Past Whilton Marina go
Long woodland stretch to Weedon
As the silent water flow

Through Stowe Hill, Nether Heyford
And past Bugbrooke, heading down
Not far to Gayton Junction, where
Some choose Northampton Town

But not our weary travellers
Where the waters will divide
Go south my friends, to Goodly Witch
Where she may be your guide

It wasn't long to Blisworth
Where community is strong
Canal meanders, quietly through
To tunnel deep and long

But when canal did open here
The tunnel-work was slow
The first attempt, it failed and so
They had another go

The walls collapsed and workers died
Deaths numbering fourteen
It's said that ghostly candles
Of those 'navvies' still are seen

'Sarpedon' entered boldly
With no fear, as in she went
No ghostly apparitions met
No dangerous event

It all went rather smoothly now
As Terry steered her through
With Perriwillow, almost bored
With nothing much to do

He started to feel hopeful, for
Perhaps his luck had changed
As not a lot had gone his way
Since life was rearranged

Emerge again into the light
Stoke Bruerne in its glory
Where trip boat, pub, museum too
All tell a ghostly story

Still, no time left to hang around
Stoke Bruerne flight, now waiting
To take them down, find Goodly Witch
Their minds and bodies aching

"What if the Witch can't help me through?
What if she doesn't care?"
The Dwarf was in a panic now
In fear of getting there

Down the locks they started
As each chamber took them nearer
To where Dwarf fate might be revealed
And make the way home clearer

The bottom lock was occupied
Two working boats were rising
'Sarpedon' stopped, let heavy load
Come through, no compromising

"You took your time in getting here,"
Said Woman, on the stern
"You should've been here days ago
You've caused us some concern"

It said 'Jules Fuels' across the bow
So 'Jules' this had to be
She called across to man on bank
"Oi, Richard, come and see"

The man he stopped and waved his hand
Acknowledged boat and Crew
"Well, better late than never
Though you're somewhat overdue

"The Witch is down there waiting
And she's worried, angry, sad
We're going to the pub tonight
She nearly drove us mad

"But now you're here, I think we can
Enjoy our pint tonight
And keep in mind," he called behind
"Her bark's worse than her bite"

So in the last lock, downward
And now mindful of the tales
It seems at last, they were to meet
The Goodly Witch from Wales

Chapter Eighteen
What Walter Did Again

The moonlit trip to Braunston
Had found 'Mr Badger' gliding
So peacefully, 'till Walter woke
And came out of his hiding

There wasn't very far to go
And just before The Turn
He spotted Perriwillow
Showing no signs of concern

The Dwarf was staring wistfully
But who knew what he saw
He seemed to stare at nothing
(Walter couldn't see the door)

Walter signalled to his Crew
That Dwarf had been espied
They cut the engine, by the bank
And glided to the side

Walter stepped down from the boat
Crept underneath the arch
That formed the bridge where waters meet
And up to Dwarf did march

"I've got you now!" the Wizard cried
"You'll run from me no more"
Perriwillow walked one step
But Walter saw the door

At second step, Dwarf reached the gate
His fear of portal grew
But Wally grabbed him round the waist
To stop him getting through

"I told you once, I've got you"
And, he wasn't letting go
'till Perriwillow elbowed him
And launched him in the flow

'twas lucky, now, that Terry saw
The scene of altercation
The team must act, stop Walter
Acting way above his station

Terry spied the 'Pusher Tug'
And 'Constance' was recruited
The urgency for all concerned
Was somewhat undisputed

Pete, he sped to action
In his animated style
Admitted that he hadn't had
Such fun, for quite a while

He jumped into the engine room
And soon the 'Tug' was running
With Terry riding shotgun
The effect they had was stunning

They sped across the junction wide
From where "The Rat" was moored
Scooped up the Dwarf, but cursing
Swimming Wizard they ignored

Meanwhile, Barry fired up
'Sarpedon', got her moving
No-one knew if they'd survive
But chances were improving

'Constance' left her precious crew
With Barry, her intent
Creating lots of havoc
With Pete laughing as he went

Round and round went 'Constance'
And she took the centre stage
As Mottley Crew got Walter out
The Wizard shook with rage

Walter jumped on 'Mr Badger'
Tried to get her started
But by then, Pete and 'Constance Tug'
Had left the scene, departed

'Mr Badger', now fired up
Was ready to propel
Though black smoke from her engine
Showed she wasn't very well

The Mottley Crew, now back on board
Prepared themselves for war
As off they went, to catch the Dwarf
And even up the score

But as we know, they were to meet
With Aemonn, weaving madly
'Kanthaka' taking all the space
Hit 'Mr Badger' badly

But as we've come to now expect
More compensation paid
As Aemonn swiftly profiteered
From mess that he had made

Walter didn't really care
Successful spell he'd found
If notes ran out, he conjured more
Then shared the cash around

'Mr Badger' smoked her way
Through locks, to Braunston tunnel
With Walter filled with one desire
- To burst 'Sarpedon's' bubble

He pushed the throttle forward
Just as fast as boat could go
Then followed where the Dwarf had gone
Now closing on his Foe

In silence, rare, they worked as one
And soon enough, they spied
The darkened mouth of tunnel, long
With Dwarf somewhere inside

Walter steered, full steam ahead
And barely missed the wall
So close in fact, his Crew believed
He wouldn't miss at all

But in they went, 'Sarpedon's' light
Shone faintly in the distance
"I'll catch you now," the Wizard cried
"No point in your resistance"

Banging, bouncing off the sides
Went Walter, at full speed
The Dwarf, in sight, had freshly fuelled
Intention to succeed

Poor 'Mr Badger' trundled on
Not built to push this hard
Her pumping pistons fit to burst
Through Wizard's disregard

But boats will always do their best
And 'Mr Badger' swam
The toughest race she'd run, though Walter
Didn't give a damn

He pushed her harder, harder still
As closing gaps diminished
"I've got you now," the Fiend cried out
"Let's get this battle finished!"

The end of tunnel now could see
The Wizard whooped with glee
"They're held up by another boat
They're waiting there for me"

But leading boat reached daylight
And the chance our Dwarf did make
He took the opportunity
Moved out to overtake

Walter wasn't happy, when
He saw Dwarf disappearing
Pushed 'Mr Badger' even more
Shot out into the clearing

The Wizard, hardly in control
Now trying to get past
The boat, with Man on Holiday
- But Walter went too fast

The Man, now seeing Wizard's Mob
Saw trouble looming near
He ran inside and locked the door
But left the boat in gear

So one boat going far too fast
The other, veering madly
And those observing from the bank
Could see things would end badly

When Walter tried to overtake
The second boat careered
Into his path, his horror grew
- It wasn't being steered!

The Wizard tried to slow his boat
As quick as he was able
(Whilst Holiday Man, he quaked in fear
Beneath the dinette table)

Walter revved the engine hard
Slammed boat into reverse
Poor 'Mr Badger' tried her best
But black smoke getting worse

She tried to turn the spinning prop
More effort was applied
As Walter pushed the throttle more
Her engine blew and died

This wasn't very timely
As collision happened fast
Inevitable accident
Left everyone aghast

The Man who was on Holiday
Crept out on hands and knees
Felt safer now, outside the boat
With maniacs like these

"Another lunatic," he yelled
"It's dangerous round here"
"That's rich from you," the Wizard cried
"At least I TRIED to steer!"

Before the row got going hard
A voice came from the bank
"I might have known you'd wreck my boat
With some foolhardy prank"

Walter and the Holiday Man
Stopped arguing and stared
For 'Mr Badger's' owners caught
The feuders unprepared

Captain 'P', on bankside path
Could see what had been done
Beside him, even less impressed
Was 'Crystal Karl', his son

"I told you not to break my boat
Just look at that big dent
And now you've blown the engine up
I'm going to raise the rent"

"Old Captain 'P', he ripped me off,"
Said Walter, "That's a crime"
"You answer now to me," said Karl
"It's compensation time"

When Captain 'P' explained the tale
Not such a big surprise
That Man who was on Holiday
Decided to get wise

So Walter started counting cash
To even up the score
At one point, had to go inside
And magic up some more

A happy man, no maniacs left
And richer than he started
Our Man on Holiday set off
And to the pub departed

Once 'Mr Badger' safely moored
Karl happy now he'd seen her
He drove the Wizard and his Crew
Down to a big marina

Whilst Walter rode in transit van
(Large fee he had to find)
The Mottley Crew feared for their lives
In trailer, towed behind

At Whilton, where large brokerage
Supplied another craft
This time, a widebeam, long and slow
- Onlookers stood and laughed

It only spelled disaster
As he'd never catch his prey
For Walter couldn't steer the boat
And just got in the way

With compensation much increased
He banged and bumped along
Walters plan that 'big was best'
Had gone so badly wrong

The Wizard, in pursuit of Dwarf
And trying to be clever
Had slowed them down, his journey now
Was taking them forever

The journey went through Weedon
Where the bends and boats gave grief
A crowd had formed upon the bank
Looked on in disbelief

This carried on, as south they went
Through Stowe Hill down to Bugbrooke
At Gayton (compensation paid)
Follow the way the Dwarf took

In Blisworth, they arrived at last
Where tunnel must be tackled
"We're nearly there, the Witch can't help
Them now," the Wizard cackled

The Mottley Crew felt nervous
And not hard to reason why
When Walter entered chasm dark
In widebeam, they might die

They ducked inside, he aimed the boat
By miracle shot in
Accelerated, hard and fast
With maniacal grin

About half-way, they saw a light
A boat was coming through
From other way, they wouldn't fit
- Now, what would Walter do?

Both parties slowed, at stalemate now
As neither could go on
They stopped, they touched, now bow to bow
Swayed gently now, as one

Walter tried to battle on
Demand they moved away
Demand that they would let him through
- It wasn't Wally's day

He'd picked the wrong opponent
And, he held the empty glass
The mighty 'Jules Fuels' forged ahead
Refused to let him pass

"Go back," cried Richard, on the bow
"The rules are very clear
You have to book a passage and
You're not coming through here"

Walter wasn't having it
He saw no reason why
He couldn't push them from his path
(At least, he'd have a try)

He revved the widebeam's engine
'Mighty Jules', she held her ground
She wound the coalboat's engine hard
And turned the game around

The widebeam now moved faster
Than it had in forward gear
As 'Towcester' pushed them backwards
'Till the daylight did appear

Walter now was fuming
And his fists, they beat the air
Said Richard, "I'm reporting you
So don't go back in there"

'Towcester' towed her butty north
As Jules, with sheer disdain
Shot Walter such a scathing look
He wouldn't try again

The widebeam had to be tied up
As journey in remission
With Walter, last seen on the phone
For passage, with permission

Chapter Nineteen
Stella Bella

Descending at the bottom lock
Through open gates they hurried
But Perriwillow, in his haste
Now found himself quite worried

The journey had been long and hard
With troubles on the way
But now it seemed the Witch from Wales
Would meet with them, today

He didn't feel quite ready
Well, was not prepared at all
He didn't know what to expect
Felt very scared and small

He didn't have too long to wait
It happened way too fast
He looked across and there she was
The real live Witch, at last

The Dwarf began to tremble
And his legs felt weak with fright
Had no idea of what to do
Just hoped he'd get it right

Stella Bella stood, her steely
Gaze like Herons Eye
With aura of contempt, she stared
No chance of passing by

Bright dungarees would bring a smile
Her dreadlocked hair hung down
But from the stern of Kelly Ann
The face, it wore a frown

"Where d'you think you've been, My Boys?
I thought you'd lost your way
I know canals are slow
But I've been waiting, day on day

"You've had me really worried and
I feared that you'd been caught
That Walter, why, he'd kill you now
Without a second thought"

Perriwillow shuddered, looked
As pale as any ghost
Of Wizard and the Witch from Wales
Which one should he fear most?

As thoughts whizzed round inside his mind
In fear he'd breathed his last
The Witch cried "Are you going to stop
Or carry on straight past?"

Perriwillow hit reverse
'Sarpedon' reached a halt
Slid smoothly next to 'Kelly Ann'
Moored up without a fault

The boats, now lined up stern to stern
And Dwarf met Witch's gaze
He hadn't got a thing to say
Now faced with eyes, ablaze

Stella Bella didn't blink
Unwavering, eye to eye
Perriwillow couldn't speak
His mouth had gone all dry

He stuttered, stammered, found some words
To conversation make
Spat out what came into his head
"I've got some tea and cake"

With widened smile on Stella's face
"Now that's a decent start
The thought of cake and cups of tea
The way to win my heart"

Terry came out, tray in hand
With teapot, hot and steaming
The cakes and scones and buttered toast
Had Stella Bella beaming

"Now there's a spread fit for a Witch
I'm glad that you've arrived
I'd eaten all my cake and bread
Was feeling quite deprived"

She tucked into the loaded plates
Filled seventh cup of tea
As Perriwillow wondered
"Will she leave a bit for me?"

They'd never seen an appetite
So keen, as plates were finished
Till mopping butter, with the toast
Her craving was diminished

"I've left you both a slice of cake
On which to feast upon
But seems the teapots empty
Have you got the kettle on?"

Terry looked on, wearily
With empty tray in sight
He feared that he'd be serving tea
'till far into the night

Recalling now of Richard's words
His heart began to sink
He now could see why up the flight
They'd gone, to get a drink

But that's no way to treat a Witch
Who'd help a Dwarf get home
So galley bound, to make the tea
Left Dwarf and Witch, alone

And so, began the story of
The Witch and how she came
To hear of Perriwillow's plight
His wish to clear his name

So holding court beside the fire
Her story to relate
Stella Bella talked and talked
Of magic, life and fate

Of how she came from far off land
With Wizards, Witches, wands
Where Goodly Folk, they fought the wrath
Of no good Vagabonds

As children, they had gone to school
To learn spell-driven craft
Where Walter, bottom of the class
Had failed, whilst others laughed

So Walter grew a nasty streak
A chip upon his shoulder
Developing his evil ways
With tactics ever bolder

But Walter had a weakness
It was Stella Bella's friend
He stared at her, with widened eyes
In love, without an end

Agnes Eleanora
Was his match in evil charm
Together, they would rule the world
Cause havoc and alarm

But often, as the case may be
Intention sometimes strays
They turned their hate upon themselves
And went their separate ways

Neither ever loved again
Each chose a new direction
But still remaining best of friends
An evil intersection

Agnes lived upon a boat
She filled with spell and potion
Whilst Wally followed her around
Still full of true devotion

The Wicked Witch, as she was known
Cast spells with genius mind
And Wally, never any good
Still followed close behind

Then enter Dwarf, meet Stella Bella's
Friend in all her glory
"And Walter thinks you killed her
Tragic end to his love story"

Perriwillow shouted out
"She killed herself with stew!
I don't know why it happened
What a stupid thing to do"

"I know she did," said Stella
"And I'd warned her of that spell
But Agnes wouldn't listen
Or believe I meant her well

"She wrote it many years before
To stop a thieving bunch
Upend the pot on Mottley Crew
Who tried to steal her lunch

"It seems that when you ventured near
To smell the steaming pot
As you ran off, the spell kicked in
And killed her, on the spot"

Perriwillow, silenced
Now the facts had come to light
He didn't know quite what to say
Or how to put things right

He'd like to comfort Walter
And to help him with his grief
Whilst Terry and the Witch looked on
In total disbelief

"But Walter aims to murder him,"
Said Man to Witch, with dread
"He thinks that sharing tea and cake
Will make them friends, instead?"

Said Stella, "Dwarf has lost his head
If friend he thinks he'll make
So just leave Walter down to me
For everybody's sake"

Stella Bella spoke to
Perriwillow of his plan
"You've made a mess of getting home
Since journey first began

"It seems you can't be trusted
Just to keep your noses clean
You're always finding trouble
Leaving trails of where you've been

"I saw you first at Hurleston
Where the Wizard caused you strife
I would have helped, except I've got
A hectic social life

"I watched 'Mountbatten' sink his boat
But then I had to dash
Watched you escape, then off I went
An all-night birthday bash

"So let's go through the final plan
And listen, carefully
No time to waste, let's get you home
- And Terry, where's that tea?"

Many pots of tea were made
With "Terry, where's the toast?"
Or "Where's the cake?", 'twas hard to know
Which one she ate the most

By midnight, it was very clear
What they would have to do
Get past the Wizard, forge ahead
Plans didn't feel so new

Perriwillow felt confused
Not sure of how he felt
At prospect now, of going home
And hand he had been dealt

"Don't pull that face," said Stella
"It's not good for team morale
So far, you've just gone up and down
The same stretch of canal

"If Walter kills us all
You've only got yourself to blame
You have to put an end to this
Return from whence you came"

Perriwillow nodded
Now acceptance had begun
The idea that his friends could die
Just wasn't any fun

He felt so very tired
And, he shed a silent tear
With weight upon his shoulders
Knew he must get out of here

With heavy heart, he went to bed
Afraid he would not sleep
But hit the pillow, dreaming of
Appointment he must keep

'Dwarf City' called and beckoned him
The dream was warm, prolonged
Where Perriwillow must return
Go back, where he belonged

Chapter Twenty
Running Back To Braunston

On waking, just before the dawn
The final journey start
With mixed emotions, wearing smiles
Which masked an aching heart

'Sarpedon' now retraced the steps
They took the day before
So up the flight, now heading north
To tunnel, dark, once more

On reaching top of misted locks
As sun rose in the sky
Stoke Bruerne, steeped in ancient vibes
Watched working boat go by

The silent crew watch water flow
Toward their destination
Stella Bella, on the stern
Seemed full of wild elation

"Come on My Boy, you're going home
Why must you look so sad?
Just think of all the friends you've made
And journeys that you've had"

Perriwillow, unconvinced
Now felt the need to cry
"Man up, young Dwarf, there's challenge yet
Unless you want to die"

As tunnel spied, a lone man stood
Requesting them to halt
"Is there a problem," Terry asked
"I don't think we're at fault?"

"A widebeam's booked in half an hour
To come the other way"
The man replied "Get in there first
It takes them half a day"

So Terry steered into the void
In haste to motor through
(I'm sure you've guessed, the 'widebeam' craft
Was Walter and his Crew)

Just as 'Sarpedon' found the light
With Stella feeling mean
"Oi, Wally, look, we're going back
Wherever have you been?"

Walter froze, in anger, wild
It seemed he had no choice
Aborted southern tunnel trip
With hatred in his voice

"I'll get you Dwarf," he cried aloud
"I'll never let you leave"
"I didn't kill your friend," called
Perriwillow, "Please believe"

As Stella had predicted
This just made the Wizard worse
He shook his fists and crashed the boat
Which really made him curse

"Where are you going?" said the Bloke
In Charge "You're booked for south
You can't go north by turning round
Close to the tunnel mouth"

"Don't try and stop me," Walter cried
He bashed and banged the bank
Then hit a narrowboat so hard
That both boats nearly sank

"Clear off," said folk from boats and bank
"There's no room here for you
You're holding up us decent folk
Just waiting to go through"

So onward, north, 'Sarpedon' went
With Walter in pursuit
Though fact that he could not keep up
Was never in dispute

They traced their steps, from whence they came
Made progress, smooth and steady
Past Gayton, Bugbrooke, Weedon
Buckby flight, open and ready

Up and up, through climbing flight
Work paddles, push the gates
Toward the top, go on, ahead
Where Stella Bella waits

No time to stop at lock-side pub
Where some were disappointed
But top lock gates not opening
Their journey, now disjointed

"We'll have to call the Water Folk,"
Said Terry, "this needs mending
We've had a winning streak, but seems
Bad luck is never ending"

At least the pub was handy
So they didn't feel deprived
Authorities took several hours
Before the help arrived

Stella Bella paced around
She really seemed quite worried
"We need to get a move on here
This job needs to be hurried

"The Wizard must be catching up
A nasty, evil man
Please tell me that you'll fix this lock
As quickly as you can?"

"Keep your hair on, Madam"
Said the Locking Engineer
"Another fifteen minutes
And we'll have you out of here"

Of course, it took an hour
For canal time runs on 'slow'
As Stella Bella paced the lock
Until the boat could go

Emerging in the nick of time
Got clear of Norton Junction
And getting very tired now
The Crew could barely function

"I think it's time you got some rest,"
Said Stella Bella next
"Though Walter's getting close again
And bound to be quite vexed

"But if I know our Mottley Lot
Their habits will not fail
They won't resist the lock-side pub
And too much food and ale"

"But if they've caught us up," said Dwarf
Will Walter still allow?"
Said Stella, "Wally's stupid
So it's doubtful he'll change now"

'Sarpedon' moored, before the tunnel
Took them underground
With Terry worried they'd be seen
Not wanting to be found

So Stella cast a cloaking spell,
To stop those who might see
"It's no good having Witch on board
Without some sorcery!"

They slept a bit, but half awake
In case the Wizard came
Just half a day to Braunston Turn
Don't want to lose the game

Next morning they were on the move
To Braunston, on they go
The Man in Charge of tunnel called
Them through, no need to slow

They entered, gathering of speed
The headlight cut through black
As Walter, widebeam and the Mob
Arrived, no going back

Walter gunned the widebeam
Man in Charge - "You can't go in!
You haven't booked a passage,"
Walter said, "I'll follow him!"

The entrance to the tunnel
Lost some bricks, as in he dashed
Inevitably far too fast
As yard, on yard, they crashed

He couldn't catch 'Sarpedon' up
But capture getting nearer
And Walter's plans for Perriwillow
Couldn't be much be clearer

Tunnel long was ending soon
In halo of sunlight
Not very long to go before
The top of Braunston flight

But right before the very end
With Walter at Dwarf's stern
A hire boat, it entered
Past the point of no return

'Sarpedon' shot into the light
Bright sun affecting vision
And widebeam sped, as tourists screamed
At force of next collision

Walter wasn't giving up
This time was going through
And after meeting 'Mighty Jules'
He knew just what to do

He pushed against the narrowboat
Where Holiday Crew, still screaming
Looked on, as Walter pushed them back
Not sure if they were dreaming

The boats were almost written off
And really in a state
But Walter, on a mission now
Was not prepared to wait

The tourists didn't say a word
But seems there was no need
For Walter showered them with notes
Beyond their want, or greed

So Walter went, in hot pursuit
Not much stood in his way
The Dwarf would not be going home
There was a debt to pay

Meanwhile, on 'Sarpedon'
Now the top lock was in sight
They needed to descend
Before the Wizard reached the flight

But luck was with them once again
As Jenny, with a grin
A cheery wave, a bright "Hello"
Gate opened; boat slid in

The news got even better, when
They spied what was in store
For every lock was set for them
Lock wheelers by the score

They even played it dirty
And, as mischief was awoken
Intent on slowing Wizard down
They left the gates wide open

As Walter reached the topmost gates
In order to descend
'Sarpedon' reached the bottom lock
So pleased to reach the end

Barry waited, smiling bright
"My honoured friends, 'Hello'
It's good to see you, safe and sound
Not very far to go"

Onto 'Sarpedon', Barry stepped
So pleased to share the ride
As Stella Bella, drinking tea
Stood on the other side

"Would you like a cup of tea
Perhaps a slice of cake?"
Terry saw the empty tray
- "Again? For goodness sake!"

But soon, the journey would be done
And worlds would separate
Where all return to where call home
Continue with their fate

Now bittersweet, they left the lock
Past Redshaw's yard they glided
Toward Marina and The Turn
To where the worlds divided

"It's very busy," Terry said
The others did agree
"With many old boats mooring up
There's lots of them to see"

"Remember what I told you,"
Barry said, "That boats attend
Braunston Historic Rally
Well, you see, it's this weekend"

"At least I get to see them all
Before I go back home,"
Said Perriwillow, "Suddenly
I'm feeling so alone

"I'm really going to miss you all
There's so much I should fear
Like how we're going to navigate
'Sarpedon' safe through here"

So Perriwillow started through
He steered, without a fault
Until a man in 'hi viz' vest
With arm raised, called a halt

Chapter Twenty-One
Parade to the Portal

"'Sarpedon', are you going through?
You're not here on my list,"
Said John, the Man in Charge today
"Or has her name been missed?"

"I've got a meeting at The Turn
So yes, I'm passing by
I'd love to stay, but things to do
At least, I'm going to try"

"OK," said John, "But wait a while
Until there's room to go
There's those in there who aren't too good
And progress can be slow

"Please follow 'Gerald' to The Turn
Just go to where she's moored
I see that Barry is with you
So drop him back on board"

With orders done, the Dwarf moved on
And 'Gerald', they did find
Now boats ahead were bow to stern
But Wizard, close behind

They heard a shout and shout returned
Which bordered on a row
"It makes no difference who you are
You can't go through there now"

Of course, the noise was Walter
With the Mottley Crew in tow
All telling John to make some room
For where they want to go

These tactics didn't work on John
There wasn't room ahead
"You couldn't get a kayak through there
Let alone that shed"

Walter wasn't happy
As the Dwarf he aimed to get
Decided he would overtake
He wasn't finished, yet

But John was no beginner
And he'd seen it all before
"You either take a Pilot
Or I'll put your Crew ashore"

There was no other option here
So John, allowed on board
Took up control of 'Widebeam'
Where some order was restored

So let's describe The Rally
With about one hundred boats
'Motors', 'butties', 'tugs'
Parading heritage that floats

Braunston Marina was the host
Showcasing days now gone
Bands, bars and plays, for several days
Plus stalls to look upon

Some boats exceed a hundred years
Historic in their age
From horse, to steam and diesel dream
Designed to earn a wage

The hardened life of coal and steel
Some working still today
Though not an easy life
They wouldn't have another way

Though pretty look, a loaded boat
Is many tons of steel
It isn't just a nice day out
The dangers are for real

So each parade is planned and run
With military precision
If steerer told they have to stop
It isn't their decision

And off they go, the 'tugs' are first
Then 'motors', 'butties' too
'Sarpedon' followed 'Gerald' round
Together, joined the queue

As on they went, more boats slot in
A massive, long flotilla
Where towing pairs, so graceful glide
Like floating caterpillar

A slow and handsome sight it made
Our heroes at the rear
And Jenny, back on 'Gerald' now
Re-joined the atmosphere

Meanwhile, behind, with John in charge
The Mob could not attack
And just as well, for line so long
That some were coming back

Toward them came two lovely pairs
Of boats with towing line
'twas Jules and Richard, "Hello, Folks
I see you took your time"

"Cheeky things," said Stella now
"They like to share a grin
I do like pulling Richard's leg
Not many good as him"

"And look who's next," said Perriwillow
"Ruth and Richard too
Bet Walter gets upset to see
'Mountbatten', in the queue

"I don't think he got over
Being squashed and pushed aside
And when Ruth swung that buckby can
We laughed until we cried

"Two coalboat men named Richard?,"
Said the Dwarf, "Both called the same?"
Said Stella, "Well, it's easier
They can't forget their name"

Perriwillow asked her
"If same name for all the men?"
Then realised, 'twas a Stella joke
They laughed, then laughed again

"Hello folks, I hope you're well"
Said Richard 'Number Two'
A cheery smile and wave from Ruth
Then gone, they'd passed on through

They heard the threats as Walter saw
'Mountbatten's' bow, once more
"Get out the way," said Richard,
"And I've told you that before"

John said to Walter, "Rudeness here
Is having no effect
I will not have a mutiny
Now show us some respect"

The Wizard was frustrated
So impatient, with a frown
He raised his wand, John shot a look
"Just put the gadget down"

Walter bristled visibly
His anger had no voice
He knew he had to calm it down
And had no other choice

Excitement over, watched by crowds
Of people standing near
All hoping for another row
To boost the atmosphere

Perriwillow, clearly sad
At what he now would miss
Desiring much to celebrate
A weekend such as this

On the way, they stocked up with
'Gongoozler Café' cake
But soon to business, Dwarf must go
With Walter in their wake

All were feeling nervous now
The journey, still unknown
And would the portal open for
The Dwarf and take him home?

Slowly, slowly, nose to tail
The crocodile proceeded
Past the toll house, pub and bridge
With progress badly needed

Stella Bella, quiet now
Not knowing what to say
For even she, with magic eyes
Could not prepare the way

The Turn in sight, twin bridges white
'Rat' moored on other side
With 'Constance Tug', it felt so long
Since portal had been spied

The towpath, too, was silent now
Folk stood, like one heart beating
The only noise they heard
The gentle engine noise, repeating

Many boat-folk lined the bank
And such a sight to see
Perriwillow, humbled
"Are they wishing luck to me?"

"Indeed they are," said Terry
"As you've really won their hearts
They're here to wish you on your way
For here, your journey starts

"There's Pete and look, there's Malcolm
Both 'the Richards' and there's Ruth
And all the friends you've made are here
They know you told the truth"

'Gerald', still in front of them
Had stopped in bridges arch
"It's time for home, young Dwarf, me Lad"
Said Barry, "Go, quick march"

"I don't know how to free the door
Or how to beat my Foe,"
Cried Perriwillow, "Let me stay
I just don't want to go"

Stella Bella spoke, at last
"Now listen here to me
You take this windlass from my hand
This windlass is the key

"Aim boat between the arches
Where the portal you once found
Just nudge the bank, the centre bit
For gateway, homeward bound

"Now, me and Terry must get off
You must do this alone"
Said Terry, "No, I'm going too
It might not get you home"

Stella Bella left the boat
No way would she go through
On sorting of this sorry mess
Much partying to do

Along came Walter, steering now
For John had jumped ashore
The 'widebeam' sped toward the bridge
Onlookers stared in awe

Remember, Wally couldn't steer
No matter how he tried
Attempted stop, but water won
His street-cred failed, then died

He shot into the bridge's arch
Where soon he was to learn
Of 'Gerald', now, with 'widebeam' wedged
Stuck fast, by narrow stern

Well, compensation would be due
But Walter turned on Stella
For helping Dwarf to get away
Oh yes, he planned to tell her

"But Wally, why'd you use a boat?
You've made a lot of fuss
Did you not think of catching Dwarf
By car, or train, or bus?

"And anyway, just look and see
You've got too much to say
You haven't noticed, that as yet
He hasn't got away"

Walter sprang to action
As 'Sarpedon', slowly moving
With Perriwillow standing proud
His courage fast improving

The air, it hung in silence
Would our heroes stay intact?
For Walter, on the gunwale now
How quick could Dwarf react?

As ever, once things happened, well
They happened way too fast
Our Perriwillow gathered speed
Aimed boat at bank, at last

He waved the windlass in the air
Let out a battle cry
He'd come this far and now was not
The time he chose to die

'Sarpedon' nudged the bank at speed
With attitude immortal
As Perriwillow lost his nerve
At sight of shimmering portal

But thirty tons of steel, we know
Was never going to stop
Her bow began to disappear
The worlds about to swap

Our Dwarf regained bravado now
"I'm going on my own"
Pushed hard and Terry fell to earth
Now sure of getting home

"And as for you, my evil friend
Who always wished me dead
Hey Wally!" Perriwillow
Aimed the windlass at his head

Walter, taken by surprise
Such force was in the blow
It really was spectacular
To watch the Wizard go

As flying, like an arrow
From the gunwale to the water
He hit the murky, cold canal
A Wizard to the slaughter

And so, our Perriwillow smiled
At how far he had come
He'd found the Witch, made Terry safe
The Wizard was undone

But in a heartbeat, journey on
And time to leave the 'cut'
'Sarpedon' slid, from world to world
And gateway, soon was shut

Chapter Twenty-Two
Reflection on the Water

Perriwillow, feeling shocked
At how brave he had been
Could not believe the things he'd done
Or places he had been

Enjoying seconds to reflect
On how, now going home
He could relax, no Wizard here
Some time to be alone

But this was Perriwillow
And things rarely went his way
He tried to get his bearings
Hoping things would be OK

He tried to slow the engine down
As going way too fast
Much faster than he'd gone before
The water flying past

He reached down for the throttle
But the throttle wasn't there
He'd need to do a double take
No comfort anywhere

His brain was working overtime
For not so long ago
He lived in world of tranquil life
Where life was nice and slow

But in the minute he'd been here
It seems there'd been a change
High revving engine, rocket speed
It all seemed rather strange

"How come I'm on a different boat?"
He thought, with no elation
"I want 'Sarpedon' back, this thing
Is way above my station"

He started to get real again
Tried not to be insulted
'Sarpedon', now replaced, it seemed
His status catapulted

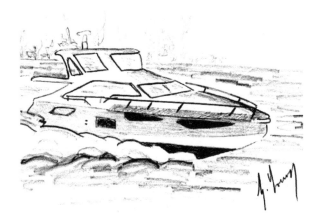

The biggest 'plastic cruiser'
That the Dwarf had ever seen
With fly-bridge and twin engines
Plus, the gadgets in-between

He somehow made the boat slow down
Somehow regained control
He didn't like this latest craft
With all its rigmarole

"It's got to be worth millions,"
Thought the Dwarf, "It can't be mine
I'm sure 'Sarpedon's' safe and sound
And things will be just fine"

At last, a proper look around
At river, long and wide
With vicious water, empty banks
It felt like suicide

A speeding launch, it pulled to port
With Gilson, his best friend
"At least," thought Perriwillow
"On this Dwarf I can depend"

"Hello there, Perriwillow
We'd been wondering where you'd been
We thought you'd gone out on a trip
A long, long way upstream

"But we were getting worried
When you disappeared from view
The river folk, they hadn't seen
Your boat, what did you do?"

And so it seemed the boat was his
He'd have to wait a while
In hope that memories return
Perhaps they'd make him smile

"Let's go home," said Gilson
"For some company and cheer
I'll race you down the river
- And the loser buys the beer"

So off they went, the race was on
And Gilson got to win
They moored the boats, 'Dwarf City Wharf'
And catchup did begin

The biggest shock was mooring up
The berths all looked the same
But one stood out, in letters large
'SARPEDON' was the name

It seemed that Gilson didn't feel
That history had changed
And only Perriwillow saw
That life was rearranged

So sitting late into the night
With need to comprehend
The Dwarf asked questions, engineered
For answers from his friend

"Do you remember younger days?"
He said, now sounding wistful
"Before I got 'Sarpedon'
And my money, by the fistful?"

Gilson, now reflective, said
"I know your life was hard
And who'd have guessed? Your fortune changed
By turning of a card"

So Perriwillow found his past
As history unfurled
Seemed fortunes changed, both here and there
To match the tandem world

Turns out that he'd been walking
And he'd had a beer or two
Got lost along the riverbank
As Dwarves are prone to do

He stumbled on a clearing
Where a wooden cabin stood
Some 'Gangster' types were playing cards
This didn't feel so good

One of the Mobsters spied the Dwarf
"You'd best get over here
We're short on numbers, sit you down
And help yourself to beer"

They gave him chips to start him off
And money started flowing
Perriwillow, terrified
Now felt he should be going

"But you're not leaving, Dwarf Me Lad,"
A rough, old Gangster said,
"I want to win my money back
You're far too much ahead"

So Perriwillow had to stay
But seemed he could not lose
The Gangster, so wound up
He seemed about to blow a fuse

"I'm going to give you one last chance
My boat is on the line
I'm sure you're lucky streak's run out
And fortune will be mine"

Perriwillow tried to lose
But cards are down to fate
The final deal, of final hand
And then, it was too late

The Gangster lost his temper then
And called the Dwarf a cheat
The others knew it wasn't true
It was a fair defeat

The Man stood up and drew a knife
The Dwarf he tried to run
The Man, he tried to follow him
It wasn't any fun

Perriwillow tripped and fell
Rolled over, banged his head
The Man tripped over Dwarf on floor
Fell on the knife and – dead!

An awful feeling, Deja-vu
Came over Dwarf on hearing
He knew a similar 'story', where
Dwarf met a Witch, in clearing

"What shall we do?" the Dwarf cried out
"He died by his own knife
I have his money in my hand
Should I fear for my life?"

"It's best you scarper, Little Man
It's not your fault he died
You won the money, fair and square"
A kindly Mobster sighed

So Perriwillow went to ground
Digesting of both tales
Of Terry and the old canal
And of the Witch, from Wales

What of 'Sarpedons' 'One' and 'Two'
The windlass he did find
The teapot and the bag of cake
That someone left behind

And what about his younger life?
His history, different now
What happened in the other world
Had changed them both, somehow

Of lives which ran in tandem worlds
Which had a similar plot
Returning, richer than he went
From trouble he begot

He slept a lot, he walked a lot
Got used to being wealthy
No Evil Fiends did track him down
His life seemed really healthy

So Perriwillow settled down
Content as life could be
He didn't have to work at all
And happy to be free

The river came to be his friend
'Sarpedon', he could steer
It wasn't very long before
Twin engines held no fear

They partied on the fly-bridge
Many friends, all good and true
But often, he reflected
On canal and all its Crew

The windlass hung upon the wall
The teapot, pride of place
And sometimes, he was wistful
With a smile upon his face

Then one day, he decided
On a trip, way up the river
And thinking where he'd like to go
His senses, all aquiver

He said he'd be away awhile
Told Gilson not to worry
And Perriwillow, suddenly
Felt need to leave in hurry

He checked 'Sarpedon's' engines
Just as he'd been taught to do
Reflecting, it was easier
With one engine, not two

Then picking up the windlass
As his heart began to ache
Heard lilting voice, of Welsh descent
"And don't forget the cake"

Glossary

'21'	The Wolverhampton '21' flight of locks
'BCN'	Birmingham Canal Navigation
'BMC'	Engine - British Motor Corporation
'BT' Offices	British Telecom Offices
Buckby Can	Special bucket for carrying water
Butty (Butties)	Unpowered boat tied alongside or towed
By-wash	Overflow for excess water level
Cill	Shelf supporting top gates
Charity Dock	Boatyard, known for 'scrap'
'Cut'	Canal (man-made inland waterway)
Dinette Table	Table which converts to a bed
Flight	A series of locks
Fly Boats	Historic 'Express' boats, worked 24/7
Fly-Bridge	Steering position, cabin at top of boat
Gongoozler	Spectator
Gunwale (Gun-al)	Ledge between hull & cabin sides
Hatch	Boat door on side of cabin
JP2	Vintage Lister Engine
'Jobsworth'	"It's more than my job's worth"
Lock	A means of raising & lowering boats
Lock Wheeler	Crew who are helping with the locks
Mooring Bollard	Post used to secure mooring ropes
'Motor'	'Motor' boat with engine
Narrowboat	Narrow enough for all UK inland water
Narrow Lock	Wide enough for a single narrowboat
Navvies	Construction workers on canal
Paddle	Means of controlling water flow in lock
Passage	Widebeams book for '2 way' tunnel
Pig Iron	Brittle smelted iron from blast furnace
Plastic Cruiser	Fibreglass (GRP) boat
Stop Lock	Historic toll lock
Tiller Bar	"Steering stick" – push to operate
Tug	Boat designed to pull or push others
Widebeam	Boat too wide for narrow lock use
Wide Lock	2 narrowboats wide or 1 widebeam
Windlass	Lock paddle winding handle
Yard	Imperial measure. =0.914 of a metre

Acknowledgements – The Boats & Their Keepers
In order of appearance

Sarpedon
Terry Glover

Mountbatten
Chamberlain Carrying Company (Richard and Ruth)

Captain Cargo
Malcolm Burge

Tardebigge
Bernard Stone

Annie Rose
Colin Wager (Captain 'P')

Mr Badger
Karl Wager (Crystal Karl)

Gerald
Barry and Jenny Wood

The Rat
Pete Boyce

Constance
Steered by Pete Boyce
Owned by Janul

Kanthaka
"Aemonn"

Towcester and Bideford
Jules Fuels (Jules and Richard)

The Parade 'Pilot'
John Boswell

The Author
Janul

Janul grew up in the Black Country, living in Quarry Bank, UK and grew up surrounded by derelict canals. Much has changed.

Writing from the age of 12, including songs, poetry, and shows, the tale of Perriwillow was born in 1980 and loved by all who read the draft. Janul had no idea where the tale would lead and had to wait nearly 40 years for her canal experiences to fill the gaps.

After suffering the day job for most of her life and by now living full time on the canal, Janul escaped the rat race and took her place on the UK canals, working on and owning a variety of boats, which indulged her lifelong passion.

In 2019, it took a year to finally tackle the story, which showcases many of the Author's friends and their boats, including Terry, owner of Sarpedon. It was, indeed, he who taught her to steer a narrowboat, way back in 1980.

Janul can be seen with her boats, Storm, The Crimson Pirate, BCN 108 and occasionally, with the truly, unruly Constance.

Illustrated by Gary Young
NB Bealtaine